Art and Propaganda
in the Twentieth Century

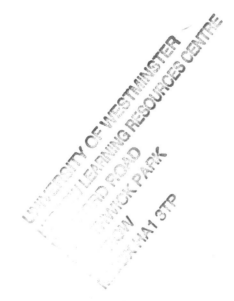

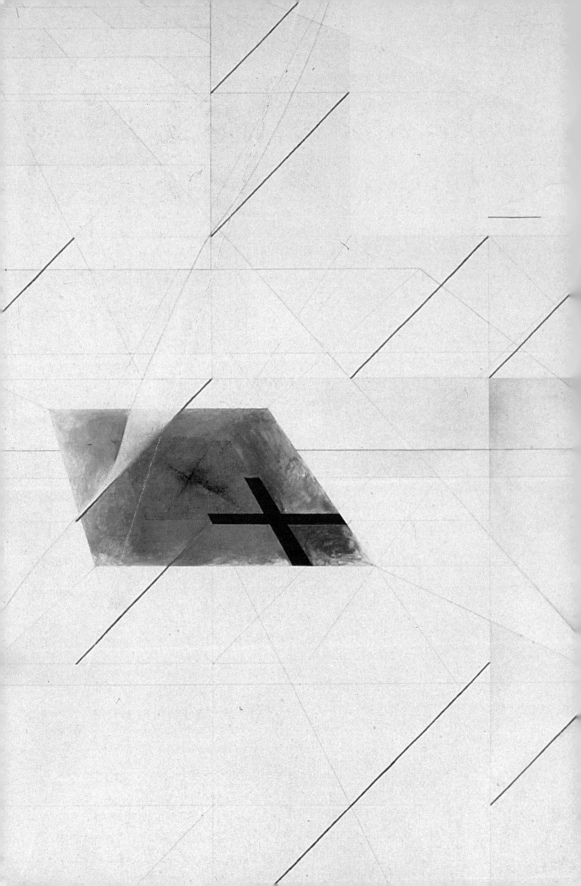

Art and Propaganda in the Twentieth Century

The Political Image in the Age of Mass Culture

Toby Clark

The Everyman Art Library

Acknowledgements

Many people have made this book possible. I must thank the staff of the libraries, museums, archives, and galleries who provided pictures and information. For invaluable advice, I am grateful to Tim Barringer, Rafael Denis, Peter Jones, Emma Kay, and Simon Ross. Chris Horrocks and Mike O'Mahony generously showed me their unpublished writings on art and propaganda. My editors, Jacky Colliss Harvey, Kara Hattersley-Smith, and Lesley Ripley Greenfield provided creative support. I am immensely indebted to Susan Bolsom-Morris for her skilled and dedicated picture research, and to Brandon Taylor who read the manuscript and made many enlightening suggestions. I am also grateful to the students of Winchester School of Art, who have taught me a great deal about art history. And for special help and guidance, I thank Joanna Price, and my parents, Paul and Frances.

First published in Great Britain in 1997 by
George Weidenfeld and Nicolson Ltd
The Orion Publishing Group, Orion House
5 Upper St Martin's Lane
London WC2H 9EA

A catalogue-in-publication record for this book is available from the
British Library

ISBN 0297 83615 3

Copyright © 1997 Calmann and King Ltd
This book was produced by Calmann and King Ltd, London

Series Consultant Tim Barringer (University of Birmingham)
Senior Editor Kara Hattersley-Smith
Designer Karen Stafford
Picture Editor Susan Bolsom-Morris
Printed in Hong Kong

Frontispiece RITA DONAGH *Evening Papers (Ulster 1972–74)*, page 157 (detail).

Contents

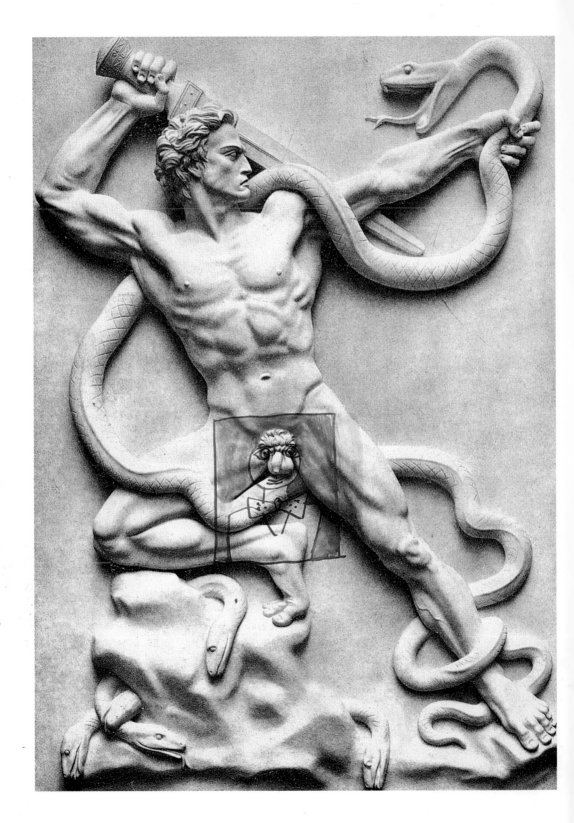

Introduction

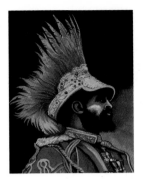

T he word "propaganda" has a sinister ring, suggesting strategies of manipulative persuasion, intimidation and deception. In contrast, the idea of art implies to many people a special sphere of activity devoted to the pursuit of truth, beauty and freedom. For some, "propaganda art" is a contradiction in terms. Yet the negative and emotive connotations of the word "propaganda" are relatively new and closely bound to the ideological struggles of the twentieth century. The original use of the word to describe the systematic propagation of beliefs, values or practices has been traced to the seventeenth century, when Pope Gregory XV named in 1622 the *Congregatio de Propaganda Fide* (Congregation for the Propagation of the Faith), a missionary organization set up by the Vatican to counteract the rival ideas of the Protestant reformation. During the eighteenth and nineteenth centuries the word was in use in most European languages as a more or less neutral term which referred broadly to the dissemination of political beliefs and also to religious evangelism and commercial advertising.

The neutrality of the word "propaganda" was lost in the First World War, when the collision of obsolete infantry tactics with advanced military technology – especially the machine gun and fast-loading artillery – killed soldiers in such large numbers that traditional methods of recruitment were no longer adequate to replace them. The governments at war were required to view public opinion as a matter of national importance, and through the developed media of mass communication such as cheap newspapers, posters, and cinema, individuals became aware of being addressed by the message-making institutions of the state on a more or less daily basis. The wartime perception of propaganda's links with censorship and misinformation was compounded by its

1. WILLI BAUMEISTER
Arno Breker's "The Avenger" with Head drawn by Willi Baumeister, c. 1941. Head, 2 x 1³/₄" (5 x 4.5 cm). Archiv Baumeister, Stuttgart.

increased application as psychological warfare waged against the morale of enemies. After the First World War, government propaganda continued in democratic countries, though official agencies now preferred to refer to it with euphemisms such as "information services" or "public education." This avoidance of the word, caused by a new sense of its incompatibility with the ideals of democracy, meant that "propaganda" was increasingly associated with the emergent one-party states, such as Soviet Russia from 1917 or Nazi Germany from 1933, which both used it unashamedly in official terminology. In the Western democracies "propaganda" became linked with "totalitarianism," a largely polemical term, which until 1945 was used in the main to describe fascist dictatorships and thereafter, during the Cold War, was frequently applied to the Soviet Union and other communist states.

The present-day connotations of "propaganda art" in the West were to a great extent shaped in the Cold War climate of the United States. From the mid-1940s, New York emerged as the leading centre of modern art, just as the United States now led the world economy. The dominant artistic values of the period were most influentially voiced by the critic Clement Greenberg (1909-94), who since 1939 had warned against the corrupting effects of what he called "kitsch," which he saw both in American mass culture and in the populist official art of Nazi Germany and the Soviet Union. To defend true art against this, artists should attend to purely artistic concerns; to make, in effect, abstract art which would be immune to political exploitation. The idea that the artistic imagination should remain uncompromised by ideological commitments was not new, but, as argued by critics such as Greenberg in the decades which followed the Second World War, the view gained a special force by its reiteration throughout a growing system of museums, galleries, and publications devoted to modernist art. These supported a persuasive historical account which implied that the highest achievements of Western art since the mid-nineteenth century were the result of art's liberation from its traditional patron groups: church, monarchy, aristocracy, and government. Freed from serving these patrons, art could be devoted to the progressive development of its formal qualities and paid for by consumers who appreciated artistic innovation as evidence of the natural creativity of the human spirit.

By the 1950s, the American school of Abstract Expressionists, among them Greenberg's friend Jackson Pollock (1912-56), was upheld as the epitome of this pure and free art. In retrospect, the fate of Abstract Expressionism can hardly surprise us: At the height of the Cold War, it was snapped up by a programme of state propaganda. The numerous international exhibitions which exported Abstract Expressionism were coordinated by New York's Museum of Modern Art (MoMA) in the late 1940s and 1950s and accompanied by curators' statements in which nationalist rhetoric contrasted the "mark of freedom" in American painting with the regimented kitsch of Soviet communism. The realization that some of these exhibitions had been secretly funded by the CIA, a fact widely known by the mid-1970s, made a deep impression on a generation of artists and critics radicalized by the Vietnam War and the Civil Rights movement, some of whom challenged the idea that art should or even *could* remain separate from political concerns. Among these was the critic Lucy Lippard (b. 1937), who in 1980 wrote an article for the feminist magazine *Heresies* called "Some Propaganda for Propaganda." She argued for the rehabilitation of the word, and encouraged artists to try to make "good propaganda": "Such a 'good propaganda' would be what art should be – a provocation, a new way of seeing and thinking about what goes on around us." This positive use of the word has not caught on widely, but the question of whether art can be both political and "good" remains a live issue for contemporary artists.

Beyond the controversies provoked by modern notions of propaganda, the use of art in the service of politics has a deep and enduring history. Rulers of the city-states, kingdoms, and empires of the ancient world used art on a monumental scale to reiterate their power, glorify their victories, or to intimidate and defame their enemies. The political symbols and rituals of imperial Rome were highly elaborate under the first- and second-century emperors, whose images were commemorated in monumental statues and a flow of coins and medals distributed throughout the empire. Architectural spaces in Rome were designed for spectacular ceremonies of triumph, obedience and unity, and for parading the booty and captives of war.

Throughout the Middle Ages, art was closely bound to politics because the spheres of religious and worldly authority were largely indivisible. Medieval works of art that ostensibly represented Christian themes were often intended primarily to support the ideological interests of the church bodies or secular powers who commissioned them. Under these conditions, the artist's aims were invariably subsumed within those of their patrons. From the early sixteenth century, particularly in Renaissance Italy, a few artists achieved personal fame, but even the most celebrated were sometimes required to use their skills to design their masters' political accessories, such as heraldic devices for banners, clothing, and armour.

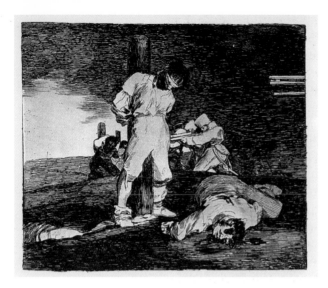

2. FRANCISCO DE GOYA
And There's No Help for It
(Y no hai remedio), from
Disasters of War, plate 15,
c. 1820. Etching, 5¹/₂ x 6⁵/₈″
(14.2 x 16.8 cm).

The idea that artistic production might be motivated by the artist's own political convictions barely existed until the late eighteenth century. The French painter Jacques-Louis David (1748-1825) stands out as an early example of an artist who chose to unite his aesthetic and political principles. He fervently propagated the ideals of the French Revolution, painting portraits of its leaders and designing its pageants. He also became a powerful politician in his own right, though he was imprisoned for his activities after the fall of his hero, the French revolutionary Robespierre (1758-94).

In contrast, the work of David's contemporary Francisco de Goya (1746-1828) exemplifies that of an artist painfully divided by the transition between traditional and modern conceptions of the artist's role. Goya had been appointed First Painter to the King of Spain in 1799, and as a court artist he made portraits of Charles IV and other members of the Spanish and Bourbon royalty. Yet he was also a liberal-minded intellectual, critical of the repressive and corrupt policies of his employers, and in his own privately made graphic works he attacked the abuse of power and the barbarism of war (FIG. 2).

Goya's ambiguous position was not unusual during the period of Romanticism, which lasted until approximately the mid-nineteenth century. Romanticism asserted the artist's individualism and social independence, as evoked in Shelley's famous pronouncement in 1821 that poets "are the unacknowledged legislators of the world." For the future of political art, this new notion of the "genius" had two crucial and conflicting effects. While it might imply that the artist could be a critic of society, it also promoted the idea that self-expression is the true function of art, and one which should not be reduced to everyday social or political concerns.

This conflict has reverberated throughout twentieth-century debates on the relationship between art and politics. These debates have centred on questions which are still highly relevant: Does the use of art for propaganda always imply the subordination of aesthetic quality to the message? Alternatively, can the criteria for judging aesthetic quality ever be separated from ideological values? If propaganda art aims to persuade, how does it do this? And to what extent does it succeed?

This book aims to provide an introduction to the issues of art and propaganda in the twentieth century, and to means of interpreting political images. Potentially this is a vast subject, and it has had to be approached selectively here. An initial problem lies in the implications of combining in the same book the artistic expressions of very different political ideologies; to include, for example, those of fascism and Stalinism alongside those of movements which have tried to oppose violence, discrimination and oppression. To imply similarities between them is to risk an erosion of fundamental moral differences. The inclusion of Nazi art is particularly problematic. The examples of Nazi art used in this book have mostly remained in secure storage since 1945. Any publication which puts these in the public domain must encounter questions of responsibility. The exhibition *Art and Power: Europe Under the Dictators, 1930-1945*, held in London, Barcelona, and Berlin between October 1995 and August 1996, has been one of the first to exhibit a large quantity of fascist and Stalinist art to contemporary audiences. Some people opposed the exhibition, arguing that because fascist and racist movements are still active, the art which has promoted them should simply not be shown. However, there is also a danger that concealing this evidence may only add mystique to the history of fascism.

Where it is shown, this art should be seen in relation to its context and functions, and this can be a means of uncovering the techniques of fascist propaganda and their effects. It also demonstrates that despite the extent to which these regimes attempted to control all areas of life, they never succeeded in monopolizing representation or silencing all voices of dissent. Willi Baumeister's (1889-1955) drawing on the photograph of a sculpture by one of Hitler's favourite artists (see FIG. 1) was not just an impudent joke. Under the circumstances (Baumeister was a banned artist at the time) it was a brave act which brilliantly exposed the face of bureaucratic evil hidden behind a pompous mask of heroism. Similarly, the Chinese students at the democracy demonstration in Beijing's Tiananmen Square in 1989 built their own monument to confront the state's symbols of power (FIG. 3). These dissident acts might be described as *oppositional* propaganda or anti-propaganda. But these terms, along with *state* propaganda or *official* propaganda, can be difficult to maintain in all contexts. Like many modern regimes, both the Nazi Party and the Soviet Communist Party had their origins in oppositional and semi-illegal movements. In addition, it is clear that some propaganda even for

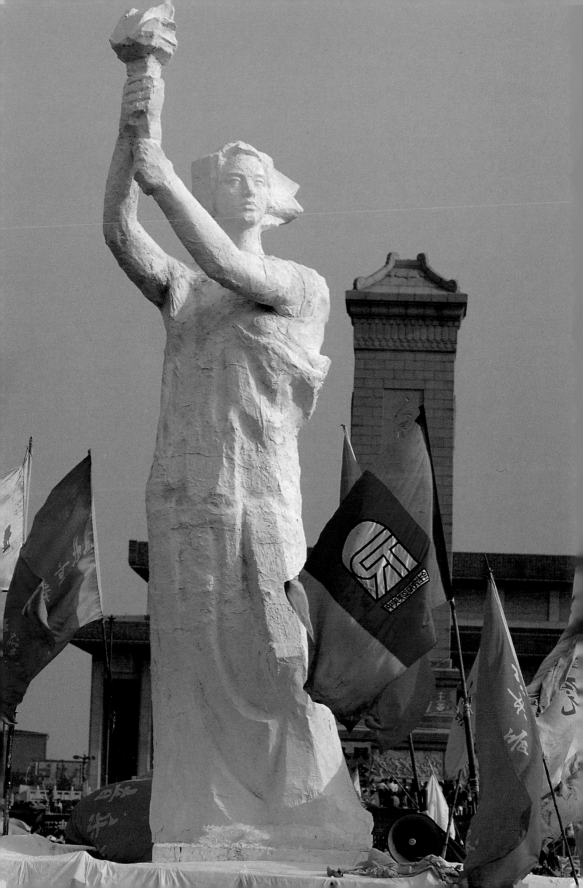

the most repressive governments was produced by individuals on a voluntary and unofficial basis.

A further problem faced in approaching this subject is the risk of reinforcing a tendency to focus on those regimes which historically have been the enemies of Western democracies. What of the propaganda of capitalism? Many writers have explored the communication of dominant ideological attitudes in the image-drenched environment of capitalist consumerism by analysing Hollywood movies, TV news, advertising, and other areas of the mass media. Viewed as a whole, these are probably too broad and pervasive to be usefully described as propaganda, though recent approaches used to analyse them can be valuable for the study of more overtly political images.

Research on the mass media has indicated the disparate and often unpredictable ways in which people are affected by images. To try to understand the meanings which any propaganda image held for its audience we need to view it in the context of other messages and activities in its viewers' lived experience. We can assume that each individual understands an image in a different way, and that sometimes the meanings inferred by viewers have been entirely at odds with those intended by the propagandist.

As in the case of Abstract Expressionism, propaganda in art is not always inherent in the image itself, and may not stem from the artist's intentions. Rather, art can become propaganda through its function and site, its framing within public or private spaces and its relationship with a network of other kinds of objects and actions. The means of making an ideological statement are almost limitless: Architecture, theatre, music, sport, clothes, and haircuts can communicate a political view, as can spectacles of violence, such as book-burning, assassination, suicide, and terrorism. The aerial bombing of civilians, which has become a routine feature of modern warfare, may often be conceived as a communicative action rather than a military one. Usually, the various modes of communication used by a government or political movement cohere to form a more or less systematic programme. And often, art operates within this system through a close relationship with compatible images in films, magazines, advertisements, popular music, and, more recently (and most potently), television and computer networks.

The history of modern propaganda is therefore intimately linked with the rise of mass culture. "Mass culture" is equally hard to define. While it connotes an old-fashioned and authoritarian idea of "the masses," it also implies the mass-production of images and messages by industrial techniques. Both Lenin in Soviet

Opposite

3. *The Goddess of Democracy,* June 1989, Tiananmen Square, Beijing, China.

The statue stood for four days while the students occupied Tiananmen Square, before being destroyed by government soldiers who opened fire on the unarmed demonstrators. The statue resembles New York's Statue of Liberty, though its face and hairstyle recall those of martyrs as depicted in traditional Chinese art.

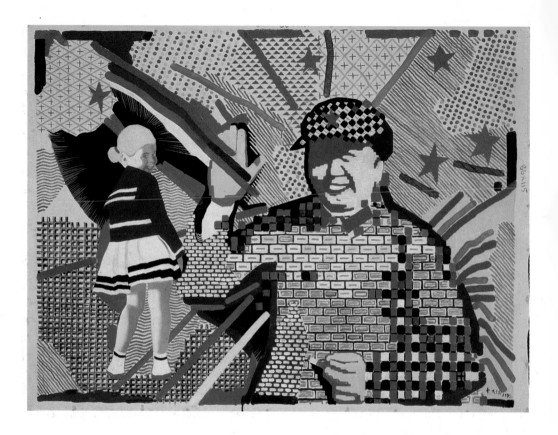

4. YU YOUHAN
*Mao and Blonde Girl
Analyzed*, 1992. Acrylic on
canvas, 34 x 45" (86 x 115
cm).

This painting parodies the
official images of the
Chinese leader Mao Ze
Dong, its mechanical style
showing up the strictly
regulated approach of
official state art. The
presence of a blond girl,
incongruous in China, is
indicative of the way Maoist
art replaced Chinese artistic
traditions with those
imported from the West.

Russia and Hitler in Nazi Germany recognized that the cinema
would be a far more effective instrument of persuasion than paintings. But they also placed great importance on art. In their different ways, Soviet communism and German Nazism were both
viewed by their leaders as movements with a *cultural* and not
just a political mission. Only hand-made works of art in the
traditional forms of painting and sculpture could fully convey the
prestige of high culture. However, under these regimes propaganda art was often produced in such large quantities and required
to conform with guidelines so rigid, that, even if made by hand,
the results could be described as mass-produced art. The painting by the Chinese artist Yu Youhan called *Mao and Blonde Girl
Analyzed* (FIG. 4) is intended as a parody or sarcastic copy of the
kinds of coldly mechanical paintings churned out in China
under the rule of Mao Ze Dong.

Artists who have opposed the ruling values of their time have
often tried to use art specifically to counteract or subvert the messages of the mass media. Yet mass culture has not been solely a tool
of authoritarian control, and images devised for mass consumption can express the views of a radical subculture. The Rastafarian

Title: Art and propaganda in the twentieth
century :
ID: 2600687024
Due: 25/11/2013 23:59

Total items: 1
04/11/2013 15:20
Checked out: 4
Hold requests: 1
Ready for pickup: 1

poster of Haile Selassie (FIG. 5) involves an elaborate overlayering of popular and high art idioms. Haile Selassie is portrayed here with a grandeur that deliberately recalls that of Roman and Napoleonic imperialism. Here the authoritarian styles of historical regimes have been adapted to provide the icons of a subversive popular movement, and one integrated with mass culture through the international success of reggae music, a powerful tool since the 1960s for propagating (though also commercializing) Rastafarian ideology.

An exploration of the relationship between art and mass culture forms a central thread of this book. Chapter One looks at radical traditions of art in the early decades of the twentieth century. Amidst the revolutionary currents of Western Europe, Marxist ideas formed the basis of debates about how art might play a role in social change. In addition to the class-based themes of Marxism, the campaign for political rights for women was conspicuous among radical concerns. The chapter discusses approaches in radical and reformist art in Western Europe and America, and reviews early feminist art and its links with avant-garde movements. Chapter Two examines art under fascism, concentrating on the art and cultural policies of the Third Reich. Although Nazism was only one version of the international manifestations of fascism, its methods of enforcing cultural uniformity and racist theories of purity and beauty were pursued with unparalleled violence. Chapter Three on propaganda under state communism focuses on the Soviet Union. Other communist states in Asia, Africa, and Latin America developed their own national versions of communist art, but often based these on the Soviet example. The chapter considers the integration of art with Soviet policies which aimed to reconstruct all aspects of social life. Chapter Four discusses wartime propaganda under Western democracies, looking at the visual techniques of recruitment, the representation of enemies, and the commemoration of war in recent memorials. Chapter Five, on the art of protest since the Vietnam War, explores contrasts and common themes in dissent and subversion in art from the late 1960s to the present day.

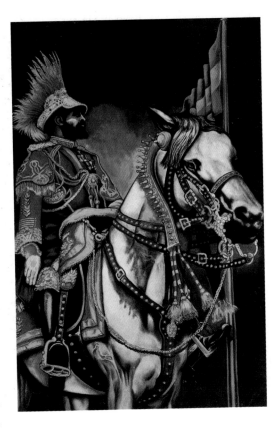

5. PETE JAMAAL
Rastafarian poster of Haile Selassie, 1980s.

Since emerging in the West Indies in the 1930s, during the rise of Black Consciousness and Pan-African movements, Rastafarianism has adopted the spiritual leadership of *Leul Ras* (Prince) Haile Selassie, Emperor of Ethiopia from 1930 to 1974. For Rastafarians, Ethiopia (never fully colonized by Europe despite Mussolini's invasion supported by the British in the 1930s) symbolizes a future spiritual homeland in a unified Black Africa.

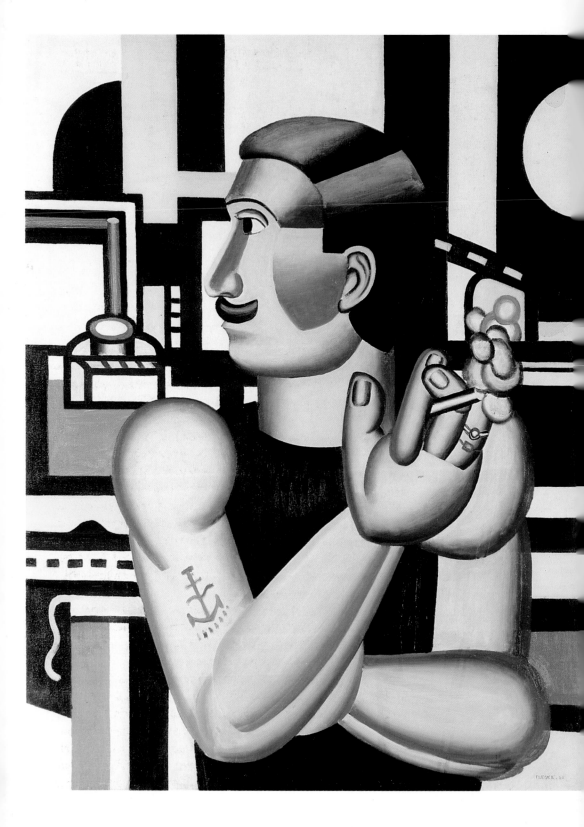

ONE

Revolution, Reform, and Modernity, 1900-1939

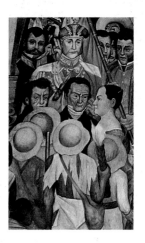

A cross the spectrum of radical thinking in the early twentieth century which embraced a shifting mixture of anarchism, socialism, and communism, Karl Marx's ideas provided the most enduring theory of revolution. In their slim tract *The Communist Manifesto* of 1848, Karl Marx (1818–83) and Friedrich Engels (1820–95) briskly outlined a compelling vision of the future of the Western world: Revolution will arise inevitably as the nemesis of capitalist modernization. The ever-accelerating rate of technological expansion, economic development, and commercial exchange cannot hold together; the energies and collisions set in motion by capitalist modernity will exceed the capacity of its forms of social order to contain them. Ultimately, bourgeois capitalism will expose its contradictions to the proletariat who, gaining consciousness, will emerge as the redemptive agent of a new phase in history.

But neither Marx nor Engels described in detail what role art might play in this process. They did not specify the topics that revolutionary art should represent, nor how and to whom they should be represented, although in their occasional remarks on nineteenth-century art and literature they indicated their general preference for realism. They particularly admired the French realist novels of Honoré de Balzac (1799-1850). During the early twentieth century, Marxist-oriented art movements adopted numerous different and often opposing approaches. The issue of realism remained a central concern, but definitions of realism became increasingly divergent. The notion of realism is complex because

6. FERNAND LÉGER
The Mechanic, 1920. Oil on canvas, 45" x 35" (116 x 88.8 cm). National Gallery of Canada, Ottawa.

it does not only imply a "realistic" style, faithful to appearances, but also an accurate perception of reality itself. Inevitably, artists differed over how the real world should be correctly perceived.

The Mechanic (1920; FIG. 6) painted by the French artist Fernand Léger (1881–1955) is clearly not realistic in appearance, but Léger claimed that his style adhered to realism because it accurately conveyed the underlying spirit of modern life. He believed that this spirit lay in collectivization, mechanization, and the rise of mass culture. The picture adapts the sharp colours and clear forms of advertising posters, which Léger viewed not so much as the visual language of consumerism, but as a new kind of urban popular art. The painting combines the direct address of the billboard poster, recently improved by new printing techniques and brighter inks, with a high-art monumentalism drawn from the public art of ancient Egypt. The Egyptian style can be seen in the simplified profile, as too perhaps can Léger's enthusiasm for Charlie Chaplin, then on view on an equally monumental scale on the cinema screens of Paris. The mechanic, a skilled worker, or what Léger called "the creative artisan," is intentionally depersonalized to imply a collective identity (though an insistently masculine one) bearing all the self-celebrating air of a film star or an advertised commodity. From his socialist point of view, Léger upheld factory-made objects as the products of working-class labour and knowledge, and sought to emulate in art their rational modes of production. Out of the dissolution of class-based distinctions between art and mass culture, and between artists and the makers of useful objects, he anticipated a democratization of cultural values which would amount to revolutionary change: "On the day when the work of the whole world of workers will be understood and felt by people exempt from prejudices, who will have eyes to see, we will truly witness a surprising revolution. The false great men will fall from their pedestals and values will finally be in their place."

In contrast with Léger's positive image of the modern hero, politicized artists in the nineteenth century had tended to depict working-class life in themes of injustice and martyrdom. These were mainly addressed to the conscience or charitable sentiments of middle-class audiences. An early example, Henry Wallis's (1830–1916) *The Stonebreaker* (FIG. 7) would have stood out to its Victorian viewers in England in comparison with more conventional depictions of rural workers, who usually featured as unobtrusive and picturesque accessories in landscape paintings. In John Constable's landscapes, for example, the naturalistic treatment of trees and clouds tends to obscure the vaguely archaic

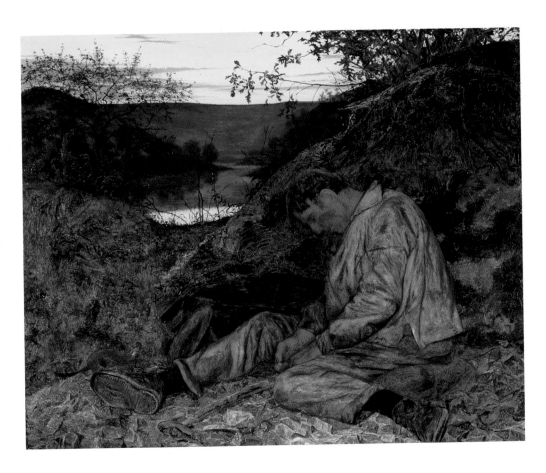

appearance of farm labourers, whose lives are sketched without evidence of social conflict. Wallis's stonebreaker is not portrayed as an example of human harmony with nature, nor as a symbol of the dignity of work nor the nobility of poverty. Instead, the drudgery and wretched isolation of the landless peasant have reduced him to the lifeless state of his tools and the broken rocks. His twisted body contrasts eerily with the tranquil pastoral setting and indicates that he is not resting but dead. To make clear its message, the picture was exhibited at the Royal Academy in 1858 with a quotation from the Scottish historian Thomas Carlyle (1795-1881): "For us was thy back so bent, for us were thy straight limbs and fingers so deformed; thou wert our conscript on whom the lot fell, and fighting our battles wert so marred. For in thee too lay a God-created form, but it was not to be unfolded ..." The painting's attention to the tiniest details – the scuffed boots, the stitches on the man's shirt – announces an ethical obligation to view and represent life with unflinching clarity. In the twentieth century this approach has been called social realism.

7. HENRY WALLIS
The Stonebreaker, 1857. Oil on panel, 25$\frac{1}{2}$" x 31" (65.3 x 79 cm). Birmingham City Museum and Art Gallery.

Stonebreaking was a common form of forced labour for work-house inmates. Wallis's painting would have been viewed as a general comment on the plight of the poor, and a specific call to reform Britain's Poor Law regulations. The left-wing newspaper the *Morning Star* suggested that "it should be presented to one of our metropolitan work-houses and hung up in the boardroom."

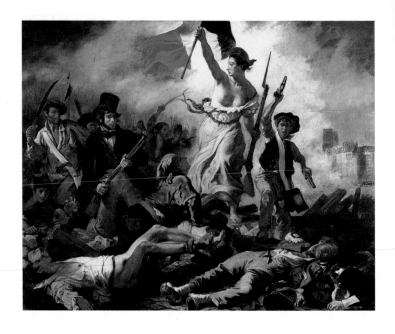

8. Eugene Delacroix
Liberty Leading the People,
1830. Oil on canvas, 8'6" x
10'8" (2.6 x 3.25 m).
Louvre, Paris.

Although political violence in the countryside was common throughout nineteenth-century Europe, the city was the main site of organized revolt. *Liberty Leading the People* (1830; FIG. 8) by Eugène Delacroix (1798–1863), which depicts the July Revolution of 1830, is the most famous painting of urban uprising, but it remains an unsettling image. The pistol-wielding street urchin and top-hatted dandy have a contemporary air that is incongruous alongside the mythic figure of Liberty, a familiar emblem in French political iconography. Delacroix may have intended to reinvigorate an allegorical convention by conflating it with a new quality of realism. The effect of this attempt to modernize history painting has been called mock-heroic, even ironic. The picture was held to be too unconventional by the French government, which bought it in 1831 but only exhibited it on a permanent basis from 1863. Although Paris had been Europe's capital for revolution, the modernization of the city in the late 1850s was designed to prevent further uprising. The slums were demolished, their radicalized inhabitants removed to the outskirts of the city, and the narrow, easily barricaded streets were replaced with broad boulevards in which the state's cavalry and artillery could be better mobilized.

Among European cities, Berlin's expansion from the late nineteenth century was rapid enough to resemble the level of hectic acceleration which Marx had believed would end in the collapse of capitalism. Its population of one million in 1880 had increased to more than two million in 1910 and doubled again in the next decade, despite the losses sustained during the First World War. The atmosphere of acute instability is conveyed in Ludwig Meidner's (1884–1966) painting *Revolution* (1912, FIG. 9) which clearly cites Delacroix's image but reinterprets revolution as catastrophe. At the time, Meidner was preoccupied with apocalyptic themes; from his imagination he painted the city being bombed, burning, or just blowing up spontaneously. He recalled the summer of 1912: "I unloaded my obsessions onto canvas day and night – Judgement Days, World's Ends, and gibbets of skulls; for in those days the great universal storm was already baring its teeth and casting its glaring yellow shadow across my whimpering brush-hand." In the painting, the face that peers up from the barricade at the bottom left is a self-portrait. Though Meidner became an ardent revolutionary, as an artist in the German Expressionist movement, which embraced a heightened revival of Romantic individualism, he mainly conveyed his political views through the evocation of the sensations of fear and alienation in the modern city. The deliberate lack of objectivity distinguished his approach from social realism. The political intention of his art lay in the aim to communicate his subjective responses as authentically as possible.

9. LUDWIG MEIDNER *Revolution (Battle at the Barricades)*, 1912. Oil on canvas, 31½" x 46" (80 x 116 cm). Nationalgalerie, Staatliche Museen Preussischer Kulturbesitz, Berlin.

In January 1919, Meidner published a statement calling on German artists to join in the revolution: "Now it must be: emancipation of the working class. But also: emancipation of the artists and poets … To the bastions of future mankind: for human dignity, love, equality, and justice. Yes we are all equal … With body and soul, with our hands we must participate. For it is a question of socialism: that is, God's order in the world."

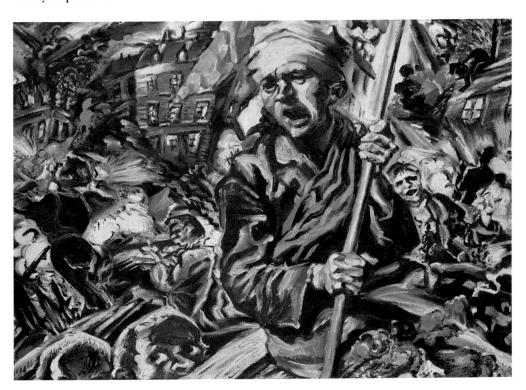

The graphic work of Käthe Kollwitz (1867–1945), who lived in the poorer districts of northern Berlin, exemplifies an approach which combines the emotional charge of German Expressionism with sober social realist concerns. Her *Mother with Dead Child* (FIG. 10) shows its subject without a context; there are no narrative details of the kind which Wallis included to explain the death of his stonebreaker. But as a printmaker, she was able to specify a meaning for some of her pictures by adding a caption or slogan and using them as posters on behalf of the socialist and pacifist causes she espoused. This technique enabled her work to move from the gallery walls, to the pages of left-wing newspapers and the walls of the street. Her style combined the direct message-bearing capacity of graphic design with a psychological intensity which made her subjects more than just stereotypical victims.

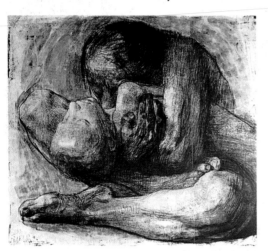

10. KÄTHE KOLLWITZ *Mother with Dead Child*, 1903. Etching, 16¾″ x 19″ (42.5 x 48.6 cm). Staatliche Museen, Berlin.

The theme of the mother and dead child obsessed Kollwitz as a private fear which was tragically realized in the death of her son in the First World War and of her grandson in the Second. Her strategy of infusing social realism with emotive themes became a widespread approach in left-wing art. But does this persuasive intention compromise realism's claim to "truthfulness?"

This question is particularly problematic where realist approaches intersect with the techniques of social documentary. The American photographer Lewis Hine (1874–1940) was an influential figure in the development of documentary photography. Hine worked as a campaigner for The National Child Labor Committee between 1906 and 1918 and within the wider Progressive Reform Movement. This was not a revolutionary movement, but one which sought the improvement of working-class conditions through legal reform. Hine's practice combined propaganda with social anthropology, taking pictures as part of a project to collect information and statistics on poverty, and as he put it, for "publicity in our appeal for public sympathy." His own sympathy for the people, especially the working children he photographed, is not in doubt, but recent attention to the ethical implications of photography has raised questions about the ideological assumptions and functions which underpin his work. His *Family in Tenement, New York City* (FIG. 11) is typical of the studies he made of poor housing conditions as part of the Reform Movement's campaign to extend the bureaucratic basis of welfare provision.

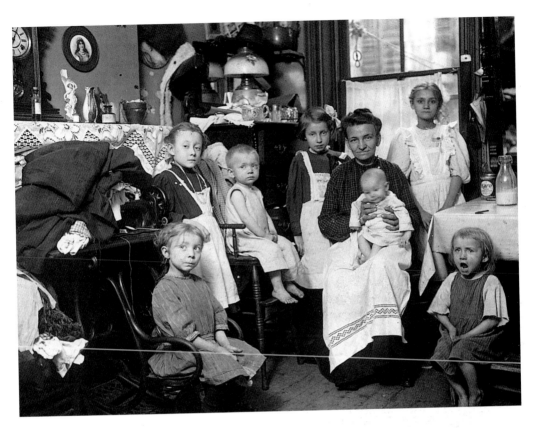

Through this photograph the spectator is brought like a visitor to the family. Most of the children look back with faces which variously suggest curiosity, anticipation, or indifference, and the mother's expression has an air of hospitality which removes any sense of intrusion or voyeurism. The family remains anonymous in the title, though, and despite the naturalness of the image, it is being shown as a sociological example. The room, the household objects in it, and the children's clothing are inspected as evidence of the family's economic and social status. There are no signs here of extreme poverty, so what is it that makes this family an object of the viewer's concern? Studies of Hine's work have pointed out how often he showed such families without a father present, using the absence of a male provider to signal the family's lack or neediness. The positioning of the spectator/photographer as filling this gap underscores the paternalistic impulse of the Reformist ideology, which tended to regard social reform within a Christian framework of fatherly care and authority. Hine's work underlines the problem for socially concerned documentary: that in depicting the poor for philanthropic purposes, such images require their subjects to conform visually with the expected styles

11. LEWIS HINE
Family in Tenement, New York City, 1910. Gelatin silver print. George Eastman House, Rochester, New York.

of "being poor." His photographs also show that realism can never be truly objective because all images are contrived; mediated through the process of representation.

Brecht and the Critical Audience

Questions about realism and about how themes of working-class life should be treated were linked to debates about how working-class audiences should be addressed. The argument between Georg Lukács (1885-1971) and Bertolt Brecht (1898-1956) during the 1930s drew up the lines between two main opposing positions in Marxist aesthetics which had begun to emerge after the turn of the century and which Marxists have battled over ever since. Lukács, a Hungarian communist critic and philosopher, championed realist art and literature of a kind which could reveal the fullness of the social world and its underlying forces in the meticulous but plain-speaking manner of the nineteenth-century novel. Modernist experimentation should be avoided. Lukács disapproved of Expressionism in particular, as failing to grasp the essence of social reality by merely depicting its surface appearances, perceiving these subjectively as fragmentary, chaotic, and unknowable. He called on artists to use art to fulfil the functions that Friedrich Engels had described: to show life as it really is and to reflect it undistorted, as in a mirror. With the novel in mind, he stressed the importance of *narrative* and *typicality*. Above mere description, narrative is the means to reveal the structures and forces of society by showing the interactions of typical characters in typical situations. In this he clashed with the views of the German playwright and poet Bertolt Brecht, whose modernism credits popular audiences with a capacity for adjusting to experimental art. Brecht argued for the need for new techniques to involve the audience in the production of meaning. If art should be didactic, it should not just impart a message to a passive audience, but provide an experience through which the audience engages and actively develops its own critical analysis. To do this, a work of art, like a play, painting, or novel, should not pretend to be a mirror in which the mediation of reality is made invisible. For the theatre, Brecht devised a special approach, his "A-effect," which he developed in plays written between the late 1920s and the 1940s, such as *The Three-penny Opera* (FIG. 12), *Mother Courage, Galileo Galilei,* and *The Caucasian Chalk Circle.* The "A-effect" (short for "Alienation effect," *Verfremdungs-Effekt*) countered naturalist conventions of theatre by openly revealing the means by which illusion is created. Brecht called this "the gest of showing." So that the audience is not lulled into a suspension of disbelief, in Brechtian theatre the scenery looks like scenery, props look like props, and acting looks like acting; that is, "showing other people's behaviour." There is no illusion of an invisible fourth wall separating actors from audience: "the stage and auditorium should be purged of everything 'magical' and no 'hypnotic tensions' should be set up." The audience should not be " 'worked up' by a display of temperament or 'swept away' by acting with tautened muscles." Brecht upheld the example of Chinese theatre in which the actor "does not conceal the fact that he has rehearsed it, any more than an acrobat conceals his training." Thus a character's actions seem not inevitable, but the result of decisions, and the audience remains open to judging the choices made and aware of the circumstances that produce or prevent alternative choices. Sometimes an actor might directly ask the audience a question, such as "What should I do next?" Brecht said that "in this way his performance becomes a discussion about social conditions with the audience he is addressing." Ultimately, the didactic role of Brechtian theatre is directed to generating a critical view of the real world, and of seeing through the illusion of the naturalness or inevitability of the existing social order and conceiving alternative conditions: "Criticism of society is ultimately revolution; there you have criticism taken to its logical conclusion and playing an active part."

Brecht developed his ideas against a backdrop of theatrical innovations in Germany which included a flourishing workers' theatre movement. By 1930 there were 150 German workers'

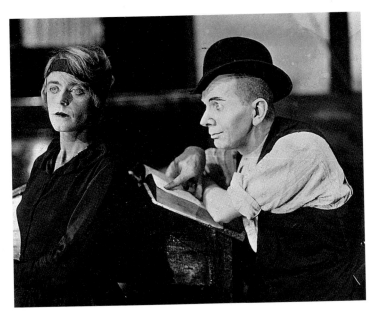

12. BERTOLT BRECHT
The Threepenny Opera,
Premiere im Theater am
Schiffbauerdamm, Berlin, 31
August 1928. Scene with
Roma Bahn as Polly and
Enrich Ponto.

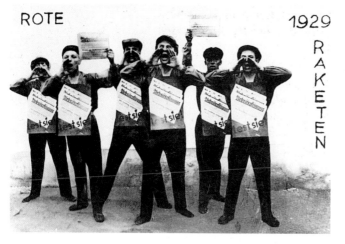

ROTE 1929 RAKETEN

13. *Red Rockets*, street agitation for the workers' press, Dresden 1929.

A communist newspaper described the Red Rockets thus: "They are shopfloor workers and apprentices, using the little time and energy left over from wage-slaving to make theatre after work. They are their own writers, directors, actors, musicians, and stagehands. Their art, and it is art, is a new growing art. Its roots are not in any particular acting school but in the life of an unbeaten rising class. What do they play? Everything that concerns the worker: scenes from his life, his daily needs, the factory, and the revolutionary struggle. Our groups are not yet the great proletarian theatre of the future but they are its seeds."

theatre groups. Some of these were travelling troupes of players who performed provocative revues using vaudeville and music hall styles, sometimes mixing them with acrobatics, songs, and jazz music. Closely linked to the communist movement, the groups put on theatrical sketches which addressed, from a revolutionary perspective, anti-war and anti-racist themes, and presented attacks on the growing presence of fascism, amidst general buffoonery aimed at the ruling order. The dramatic approach of the groups combined an awareness of avant-garde theatre and the satirical tradition of cabaret. They travelled to small towns and rural areas and also performed and recruited in factories. One of the most active of these troupes was the Berlin-based Red Rockets (FIG. 13). A Red Rockets performer declared: "Our troupes don't exist to produce 'culture.' ... Our first and foremost task is to explain with our images and scenes, satire and vivid presentation to young people what words alone leave unexplained. We must make them warm to our slogans, awaken and develop their class consciousness, their sense of belonging to the oppressed and exploited and their understanding that it is their duty to join our ranks and take part in the struggle." These theatre groups were constantly harassed by the police. The Red Rockets were banned outright in 1929, and other left-wing theatre groups were driven underground when the Nazi Party came to power in 1933. But the views of Brecht and the workers' theatre movement about the importance of audience participation have had a lasting influence on political theatre.

"Deeds not Words": Women's Propaganda and the Avant-Garde

Most radical art movements of the early twentieth century adopted class-based issues as their principal concern. But alongside these, the campaign for women's rights, especially the right to vote, was conspicuous among political struggles in Europe and the United States. Most of those who produced propaganda for the suffrage movements were not professional artists, though the implications of their work sometimes challenged dominant ideas about art. Some even took on the art institutions directly, and adopted them as the stage for political action.

The British campaigner for women's suffrage Mary Richardson did this in 1914 when she took a small axe into the National Gallery in London. She used it on *The Rokeby Venus* (c. 1650; FIG. 14) by Diego Velázquez (1599–1660), smashing the glass and slashing the painting a number of times before being restrained and arrested. She explained at her trial that her motive had been to draw attention to the treatment of the suffragette leader Emily Pankhurst, who had been on hunger strike in London's Holloway Prison. It was not an isolated event but one of many propaganda activities which the militant wing of the suffrage movement had carried out in Britain since 1905 to gain the vote and to oppose wider discrimination against women. The attack on the painting would have been partly understood as an extension of the suffragettes' tactic of smashing department store windows, which assaulted the feminized spaces of consumerism like a parodic inversion of

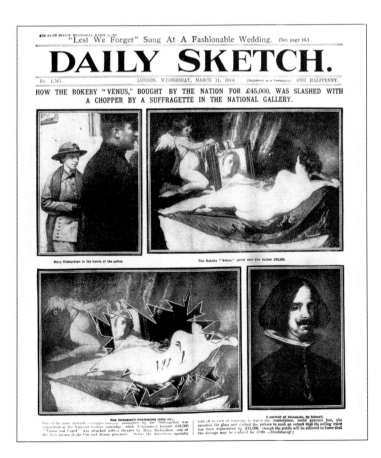

14. Newspaper coverage of the damage done to Diego Velázquez's *The Rokeby Venus*, c. 1650, by the suffragette Mary Richardson on 10 March 1914.

Drummond's uniform had
been donated by a firm of
regalia manufacturers for the
Women's Sunday
demonstration, 21 June
1908. It recalls the uniforms
of women in the Salvation
Army, though the riding crop
is more like that of a cavalry
officer. Militant suffragettes
like Drummond called
themselves a "suffrage army
in the field." By 1913
Drummond had been
arrested and imprisoned
three times for her activism.
Among her acts of protest,
she had hired a steam launch
and taken it down the River
Thames to the House of
Commons. Standing on the
cabin roof, and accompanied
by a brass band, she
addressed the Members of
Parliament through a
megaphone before being
chased off by the river
police.

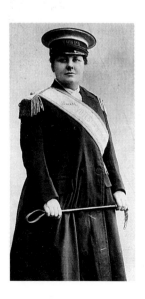

shopping. By moving the battle to the nation's foremost art museum, Richardson brought the values of the state's guardians of culture into the line of fire, and by choosing a famous picture of a nude woman, she targeted the point of intersection between institutional power and the representation of femininity.

Richardson's act provoked a complex set of meanings and effects. At first sight, it looks like an attack on the control and exposure of the female body as an object of male erotic pleasure. Richardson remarked that she had disliked the way men in the gallery had "gaped" at the picture. But she admired the painting itself, comparing Velázquez's Venus with her own political heroine, saying, "I have tried to destroy the picture of the most beautiful woman in mythological history as a protest against the Government destroying Mrs Pankhurst, who is the most beautiful character in modern history." Yet Richardson had not destroyed the picture, but altered it, making a new image – the slashed Venus – which was widely reproduced in photographs in the national press, as Richardson had surely anticipated. Though the newspapers' response was hostile, demonizing "Slasher Mary" as a monstrous hysteric, Richardson had succeeded in using the mass media to disseminate "her" picture of a wounded heroine, in effect a metaphorical portrait of the martyred Pankhurst and of the suffering of women in general.

In addition to individual headline-grabbing actions like Richardson's, the suffragettes held public rallies on a scale unprecedented in Britain and seldom matched until the American Civil Rights and Vietnam demonstrations of the 1960s. "Women's Sunday," held on 21 June 1908 in London's Hyde Park, amassed some 500,000 demonstrators. Many of them had arrived on the thirty chartered trains and marched to the park in seven separate processions. The event had been advertised with posters on buses and billboards, as well as handbills distributed at factories, shops, hospitals, and restaurants, and through the campaign offices set up throughout London. The logistical complexity of the event was stressed by the newspapers, forced to adjust their usually patronizing view of the suffrage movement; as one paper conceded, "it displayed military (apart from militant) genius to a degree that was quite astonishing." Women's Sunday marked a notable stage in the historical transformation of the art of demonstration from its origins in religious processions and evangelical meetings to its modern style of political expression.

In addition to the scale of the suffrage movement's events, the organizers carefully planned their visual effects. The movement adopted its own colours – purple, white, and green – displayed

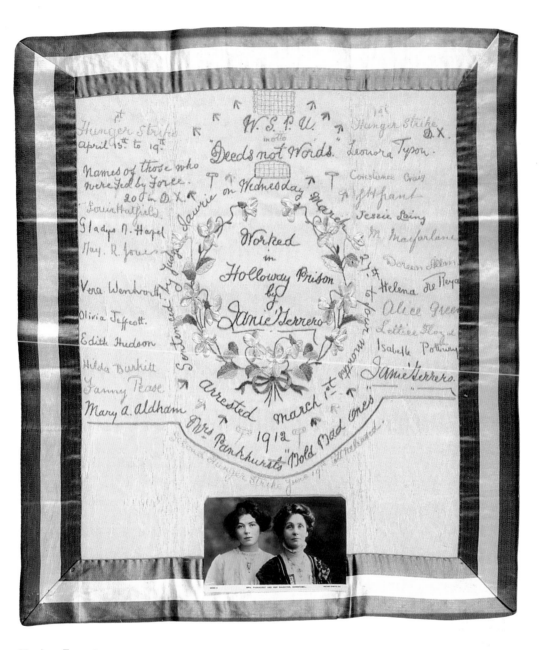

16. Janie Terreno
Suffragette handkerchief, worked in Holloway Prison, 1912. Silk, 20 x 18″ (51 x 45.5 cm).
Museum of London.

The embroidered slogan at the top, "Deeds Not Words," was the motto of the militant
suffragettes. Beneath it are listed the names of women convicts on hunger strike. The stitched
arrows refer to the markings on prison uniforms. Suffragettes on hunger strike endured force-
feeding until the British government introduced the Temporary Discharge for Ill-Health Act in
1913, by which hunger strikers were released and then re-arrested when their health had
recovered. It was nick-named "The Cat and Mouse Act."

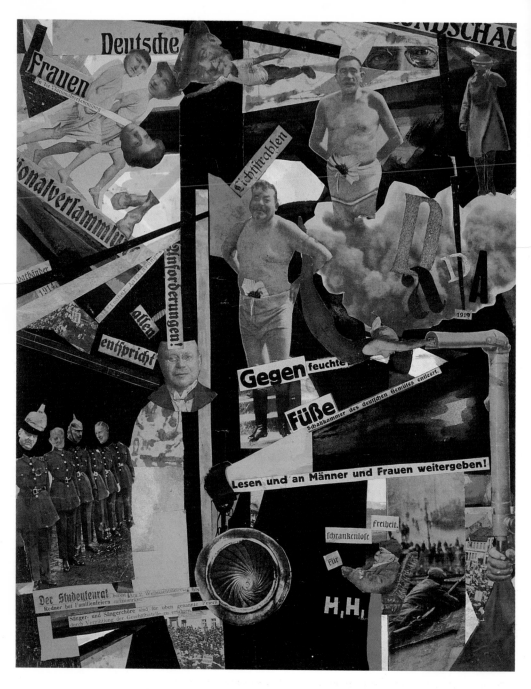

17. HANNAH HÖCH
*Dada Panorama (Dada
Rundschau)*, 1919.
Photomontage, 17³/₄ x 13³/₄"
(45 x 35 cm). Berlinische
Galerie, Berlin.

in clothes, accessories, and elaborate banners, and some of its leaders wore specially designed costumes (FIG. 15). These gave the movement a visual coherence and used fashion as a means of ideological statement. The aesthetic dimension of the movement had been developed in artistic groups like the Suffrage Atelier, which was formed in 1909 and described its aim as being to provide women with "training in the arts and crafts of effective propaganda," and to advance "the women's movement by supplying pictorial advertisements, banners, and decorations." Working collectively, the women artists practised skills such as drawing, stencilling, and needlework to produce political artefacts. They consciously disregarded the conventional hierarchy which sets art above craft and upholds the "timeless masterpiece" above anonymous ephemera (FIG. 16).

In Germany, women gained the right to vote in 1918 and the first women politicians ran for office in January 1919. The artist Hannah Höch (1889–1978) celebrated this with a photomontage called *Dada Panorama* (FIG. 17). At the top left-hand corner, the face of Anna von Giercke, an activist recently elected to the Assembly, is among the toga-wearing women shown dancing into the picture. The American president Woodrow Wilson, with a tiny body, hovers above as if to greet them. The two men in bathing suits are President Ebert and Reichswehrminister Noske, leaders of the Social Democratic Party who had been photographed while bathing at a seaside resort. Höch has given Ebert a pair of little riding boots (as a protection "against damp feet," according to the slogan) and both have flowers like feminine adornments, but also like absurd penises. Their flabby impotence contrasts with the lithe girl gymnast who dives past them, while, to the left, heads topple off the military establishment. As one of the first artists to develop photomontage, Höch made full use of the technique's capacity for subversion and silliness, creating an image of both sexual and political revolution – "unbridled freedom for HH," says the caption at the bottom.

Höch was involved with the Berlin Dada group, founded in response to the First World War and the revolutionary turbulence of post-war Germany. Communist in orientation, the German Dadaists opposed militarism, nationalism and colonialism, and amidst their rejection of dominant cultural values they viewed art itself with contempt: "Art should altogether get a sound thrashing," wrote the Dadaist Richard Hülsenbeck, "and Dada stands for that thrashing with all the vehemence of its limited nature." They particularly despised the mystical bent of German Expressionism, which, despite links with the radical left, often elevated art as a mode of inspiration or of special access to the spiritual. In this they detected the kind of obsequious sentimentality which leads to nationalism and war; as Hülsenbeck put it, "the most absurd idolatry of all sorts of divinities is beaten into the child in order that the grown man and taxpayer should automatically fall on his knees when, in the interest of the state or some smaller gang of thieves, he receives the order to worship some 'great spirit.'" They modelled themselves less as an artistic group and more as a radical cell of agitators working in the field of art, arranging inflammatory exhibitions and issuing manifestos in the name of "The Dadaist Revolutionary Central Council."

Photomontage (the combination of photographs into a composite image) had particular value to the Dadaists as a means of producing propaganda imagery conceived as a counter-aesthetic. As well as its facility for satirical effects, as in the grotesque travesties of Höch's *Dada Panorama*, its dissolution of pictorial composition resonated with the real state of collapse in post-war Germany's social order. Avant-garde circles throughout Europe were developing pictorial procedures which broke away from rules of compositional harmony and conventional ways of creating the illusion of perspectival space. Among Dada artists, linear perspective implied a rationalist system which was bound to the logical and utilitarian outlook of Western capitalism, an outlook that in their view had reduced the working classes to industrial wage slaves and had produced a deadly war machine. They also viewed realism in painting as adopting a passive relationship to the world; merely copying it, not changing it. In contrast, photomontage combined the photograph's proximity to objective reality with a dynamic process of reordering which enacted, at least metaphorically, the revolutionary reordering of society. Dadaists also liked the technique because it requires no special skills and thus overthrows the status of the artist as a trained specialist. It is said that they first encountered the technique as a hobby – a kind of modern folk art – invented by German soldiers in the trenches, who, to amuse themselves and their friends, combined their photographs with pictures from magazines and sent them home as postcards.

In her later work Hannah Höch moved away from explicit engagement with left-wing themes of class struggle and anti-fascism, and as a result she has been regarded as a "less political" artist. But recent study of her work in the Weimar period after the First World War has revealed how she retained ideological concerns which focused on the representation of women and sexuality. The 1920s saw rapidly shifting images of women in the media, reflecting the changing roles of women in society. The German press was fascinated by the "new woman," the urbanite with a salary who expressed her independence by wearing trousers and smoking cigarettes in public or engaging in sports and sexual experimentation. Höch's photomontages of the 1920s explore and reinvent images of femininity drawn from the press. Some combine parts of photographs of men and women to form images of androgyny; in one, Marlene Dietrich's legs are placed upside-down on a pedestal like a triumphant phallic monolith. At the time, this sort of intervention with media images of gender and sexuality would probably not have been viewed as explicitly political, nor as propaganda, and for Höch they related in a more personal way to her own sexuality and her long-standing lesbian relationship with the Dutch writer Til Brugman. In the 1980s and 1990s, however, strategies like these have taken a central place in feminist art and theory, so conspicuous an element in the political make-up of postmodernism.

In this context, the French artist Claude Cahun (1894–1954) has been recently reevaluated and recovered from obscurity as the "lost Surrealist." Born as Lucy Schwob to a family of Jewish intellectuals, she engaged in a varied career of art, acting, poetry, and political activism. She became involved with the Surrealists after meeting them as members of a group of communist artists and writers in 1932. At this time, there were serious tensions in the Surrealists' relationship with communism. The Surrealists, who had formed in the early 1920s under the leadership of André Breton (1896-1966), had insisted that theirs was a revolutionary movement, one that sought the overthrow of capitalism through the liberation of the unconscious; a revolution of the mind based on complete personal freedom from both external oppression and from the internal repression or censorship of the mind's unconscious life, as expressed in dreams and fantasy. From its earliest years, the Surrealist group had tried to join forces with the French communist movement, but despite temporary alliances, they were generally rebuffed by the communists, who viewed Surrealism as too undisciplined at best, and at worst as middle-class, decadent, and fatuous. By 1934, the aesthetic policy of the international communist movement was oriented towards Moscow's increasingly doctrinaire insistence that the only proper communist art was an easily legible realism expressing clear working-class themes. Opposing this, the Surrealists argued for art which could more fully incorporate the psychological life of individuals.

Cahun had left the communists in 1933. Much of her artistic activity depended on the radical transformation of her own

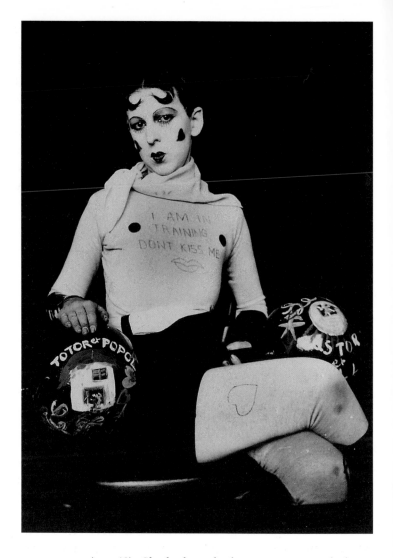

18. CLAUDE CAHUN
Self-Portrait, c. 1927. 4¼ x
3″ (11 x 8 cm). Jersey
Museums Service.

appearance (FIG. 18). She had worked on montages and photographic self-portraits since 1914 as a student at the Sorbonne,
and from 1919 she wore dramatically short hair, sometimes dyeing
it pink, green, and gold. Alongside her adoption of various
pseudonyms, her self-portraits explore a repertoire of playfully
shifting identities, portraying her as a soldier or convict with shaved
head, or as a wild parody of the Hollywood good-time girl, or
as a circus acrobat. Like Höch's art, Cahun's work was closely allied
to her lesbianism and to a practice which involved a parodic
masquerade in a series of stereotypical feminine roles which
only emphasized her adamant refusal to conform to them. Until
recently, these activities lacked a context through which they could
be widely understood as "political." As a form of propaganda, they

are certainly oblique, although at an everyday and popular level the adoption in public of a non-conformist appearance has been readily understood as a form of political statement since long before the age of hippies and punks. As it transpired, Cahun's most explicit propaganda work would be as a member of the Resistance forces against the Nazi occupation of Jersey, where she lived during the war, engaging in four years of anti-Nazi activities which included flying a banner from a church which read, "Jesus is great, but Hitler is greater – for Jesus died for the people but the people die for Hitler." She was arrested in 1944 and condemned to death by the Gestapo. Despite a reprieve, she spent nearly a year in prison from which she never fully recovered, physically or mentally.

Murals and National History

For many countries outside Europe, revolution has accompanied the emergence of the modern state out of a condition of colonialism. In this process, public art has functioned to articulate revised narratives of national identity. Mexico's revolution, initiated by an uprising against the dictator Porfirio Díaz in 1910, led to the ideological dominance of Marxist nationalism which was expressed artistically in the Mexican mural movement. Beginning around 1921, a number of Mexican muralists produced state-sponsored art which reinvented the nation's history on an epic scale. In *The History of Mexico* (FIG. 19), painted on three walls of the National Palace in Mexico City, Diego Rivera (1886-1957) depicted a vision of the nation's past and future from the perspective of the new regime. The viewer is placed physically in that perspective, enveloped by a virtual panorama which swirls through history and myth. On the right-hand wall, Rivera shows the pre-Columbian world as an idyllic era governed by the legendary god-king Quetzalcoatl. On the far left, the ongoing revolution is shown under the guiding figure of Karl Marx, who points towards a utopian future of harmony between industry and nature. Between these mystical poles, the centre wall shows in interweaving layers the effects of the sixteenth-century Spanish Conquest, leading from the bottom, where the Aztec prince Cuauhtemoc battles with Cortez the conquistador, upwards through contrasting scenes of war, work, Christianization, and education. These are portrayed as dialectical struggles between repression and resistance, cruelty and enlightenment, destruction and development. The process culminates at the top of the centre arch with the leaders of the revolution holding a banner with their slogan "Land and Freedom." Overall, Rivera's mural valorizes the revolutionary nationalism

Overleaf
19. DIEGO RIVERA
Legacy of Independence,
centre arch of *The History of Mexico – From the Conquest to the Future,*
1929–35. Mural. National Palace, Mexico City.

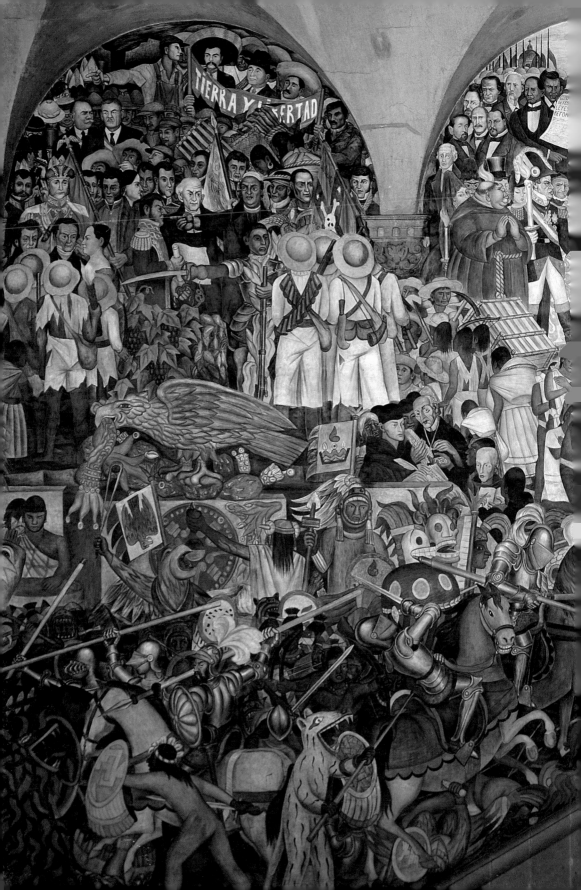

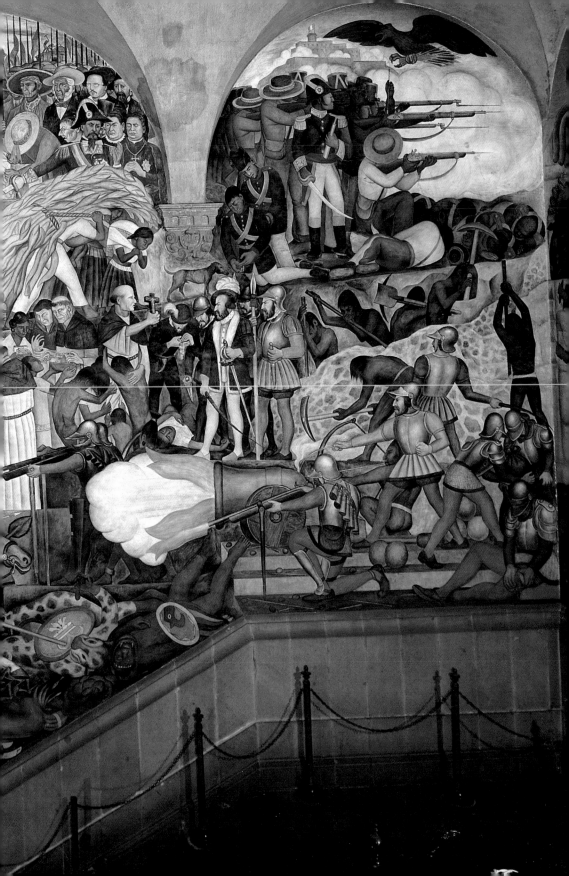

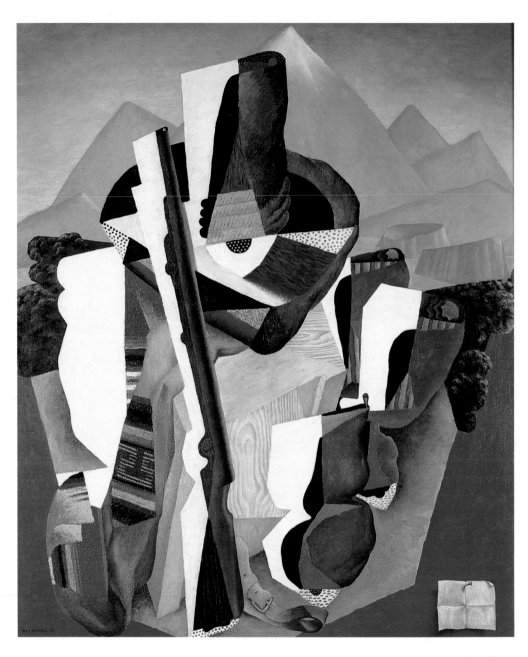

20. DIEGO RIVERA
Zapatista Landscape – The Guerrilla (Paisaje zapatista – El guerrillero), 1915.
Oil on canvas, 4′8″ x 4′ (1.44 x 1.23 m). Museo Nacional de Arte, Mexico City.

Emiliano Zapata was world-famous as the personification of the Mexican revolution. In a mixture of Cubist portrait and still-life, the painting assembles symbols of the peasant's way of life: the sombrero, the patterned textiles, the rifle, and the mountainous terrain. It suggests the *Zapatista* slogan "Land and Freedom," though also inadvertently the internal fragmentation of the revolutionary movement. Zapata was shot in 1919 in a spate of fratricidal killings.

of his patron, the government, by providing a synthetic allegory of its origins.

Rivera had developed his mural style gradually. As a young artist living in Paris, he had first treated revolutionary themes in the urbane idiom of Cubism (FIG. 20). But after returning to Mexico, he was encouraged by José Vasconcelos, Secretary of State for Public Education, to replace avant-garde interests with an extensive study of church art of the Italian Renaissance. Rivera then applied to this knowledge of ecclesiastical didacticism a vein of Mexican populism by drawing on the famous graphic work of José Guadalupe Posada, who created satirical prints for the press. For Rivera and the other main muralists, David Alfaro Siqueiros (1896–1974) and José Clemente Orozco (1883-1949), murals could address a collective audience and avoid the private and property-related format of small-scale painting. As they stated in their manifesto, "A Declaration of Social, Political, and Aesthetic Principles," published in 1924: "We repudiate so-called easel painting ... because it is aristocratic, and we praise monumental art in all its forms, because it is public property ... Art must no longer be the expression of individual satisfaction which it is today, but should aim to become a fighting, educative art for all." Their movement presented an important model for the practice of mural painting throughout Latin America and the United States, and also, from the 1960s, in countries in post-colonial Africa. But while the Mexican muralists may have provided Mexico with a national image which might help to reinforce self-respect, cohesion, and independence, they also aimed to legitimize a regime which was soon mired in corruption and civil abuses. Though barely hinted at in Rivera's paintings, the revolution and ten years of civil war had killed more than a million Mexicans.

Radical Art on the Grand Scale

Pablo Picasso's *Guernica* (FIG. 21) has been widely regarded as the highest achievement in modernist political painting. Yet it is difficult to appraise *Guernica* now without a sense that its prestige is inseparable from the unparalleled status of its creator, who when he made it was already the richest, most celebrated living artist and charismatic participant in the forging of his own image as a genius. It is also hard to assess it in detachment from the pathos of its subject and, even in reproduction, from the knowledge that it is a very *big* painting. It was initiated in January 1937 when Picasso (1881–1973) was offered a commission by Spain's embattled Republican government to paint a mural-sized picture

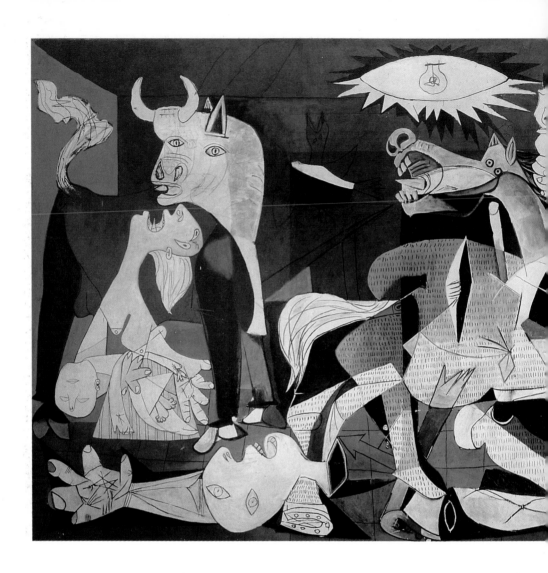

21. PABLO PICASSO
Guernica, 1937. Oil on
canvas, 11′5¹/₂″ x 25′5³/₄″
(3.5 x 7.8 m). Museo
Nacional Centro de Arte
Reina Sofia, Madrid.

for the Spanish pavilion of the 1937 Paris World's Fair. This
was the first state commission Picasso had received for a public
monument. That he accepted it was probably due to his ardent
support for the beleaguered Republic in the Spanish Civil War
(1936–39) and a general sympathy with the communistic make-up
of its Popular Front government. Though he was initially stuck
for ideas, the bombing of the Basque town of Guernica some four
months later provided him with his topic.

Even by the standards of modern warfare the incident marked
a stunning level of arbitrary brutality. The attack on an undefended
town of no military significance was apparently ordered from Berlin
and was carried out by squadrons of the German Condor Legion
on behalf of the fascist antigovernment rebels. They bombed

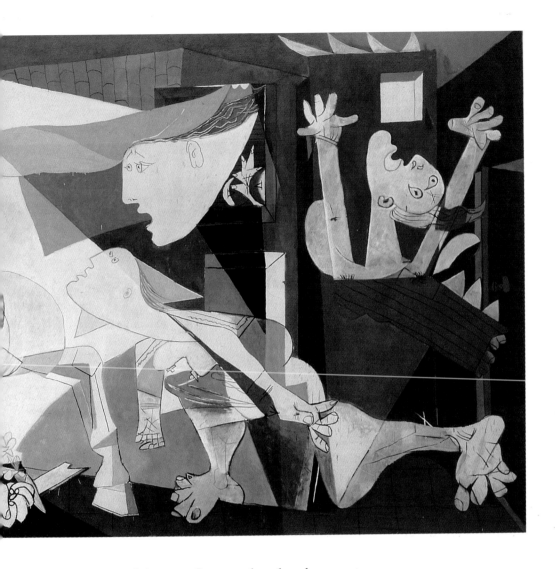

and machine-gunned the town for more than three hours, ostensibly aiming for a bridge, the only strategic target, which they missed, destroying instead 70 per cent of the town, the ruins of which burned for three days. The Nationalist press of Francisco Franco (1892-1975), the fascist rebel leader, claimed that the town had not been bombed at all, but dynamited by retreating communists, a story repeated in conservative French newspapers. In 1946 Hermann Göring remarked off the record during the Nuremberg Trials that this high-density aerial bombardment, the first *Blitzkrieg*, had been mainly conceived as a training exercise. Though only one of innumerable war crimes committed by both sides in the Civil War, the incident seems specially marked out for the kind of bewildered outrage conveyed by Picasso's painting.

The Paris World's Fair, mounted in the waning years of European peace before the Second World War, was a showpiece event oriented towards trade and popular entertainment. It was also a major site for the playing out of ideological rivalries in art and design, particularly evident in the gigantic pavilions of Nazi Germany and the Soviet Union, which confronted each other in an architectural glowering match. For other countries, it was a time of transition in left-wing positions on aesthetics. Though communist art in the West was largely dominated by realist tendencies, the Popular Front, an international organization launched from Moscow in 1935, sought to expand the communist platform abroad by encouraging a more pluralistic constituency to include modernists and liberal sympathizers under the common cause of anti-fascism (although inside the Soviet Union cultural policy was increasingly restrictive). *Guernica* was received as an important statement for this new politico-cultural alliance. Some communist critics rebuked Picasso for not including in the painting a clear pro-communist message – he had in fact considered doing so, having included in two early studies the clenched fist of the Republican salute, one version holding the communist symbol of the hammer and sickle. But although Picasso had suppressed this motif in the final version, most Popular Front critics agreed to acclaim the painting.

Picasso himself described *Guernica* as a work of deliberate propaganda, adding that it was the only example of propaganda art in his career – though he later worked on imagery against the Korean War, and as an open Communist Party member after the Second World War, he drew a portrait of Stalin. But he was not clear in stating what, precisely, his picture meant. It is evidently an allegorical or symbolic work, but what do its elements symbolize? The bull has been assumed to represent Franco or fascism, and the horse to symbolize the Republic or "the people," though Picasso was reluctant to confirm these interpretations. In using these motifs he had barely deviated from his imagery of the 1930s, which had mainly elaborated on private themes, with no obvious political intent. In his use of bullfighting motifs, the bull had appeared as an ambiguous symbol of aggression and passion, often erotic, with strong suggestions of self-portraiture in tune with Picasso's tendency to histrionic representations of his sexuality. Imagined images of violence against women had also recurred in his earlier work.

Those who criticized the painting from a left-wing and anti-modernist position described it as too vague; these critics would have preferred a more literal and realistic image which could

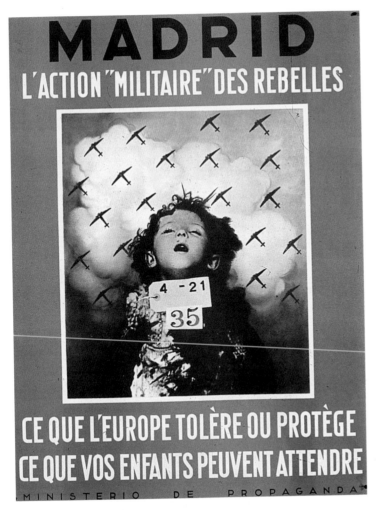

MADRID
L'ACTION "MILITAIRE" DES REBELLES

4 - 21
35

CE QUE L'EUROPE TOLÈRE OU PROTÈGE
CE QUE VOS ENFANTS PEUVENT ATTENDRE
MINISTERIO   DE   PROPAGANDA

22. *Madrid – Military Action of the Rebels (Madrid – L'Action "Militaire" des Rebelles),* c. 1937. Poster. Musée de la Publicité, Paris.

communicate its meaning and its political position more clearly. It is true that the intended meaning of *Guernica* is dependent on its title and context, but this reliance on text and site is not uncommon (nor specifically modernist) in propaganda. A large proportion of propaganda posters, for example, would lack a clear meaning without their written slogans, and some of these are incomprehensible when removed from their context. Propaganda images are seldom devised to communicate independently, and accordingly, *Guernica* was designed to be understood alongside a broad set of Spanish Civil War images, especially the widely distributed press photographs and newsreels. The black and white scheme of the painting sets up a comparison with these, and at the time its success was partly judged against them. Is *Guernica* more or less effective than the contemporary poster (FIG. 22) which shows a photograph of a dead child? A simple "objective" revelation

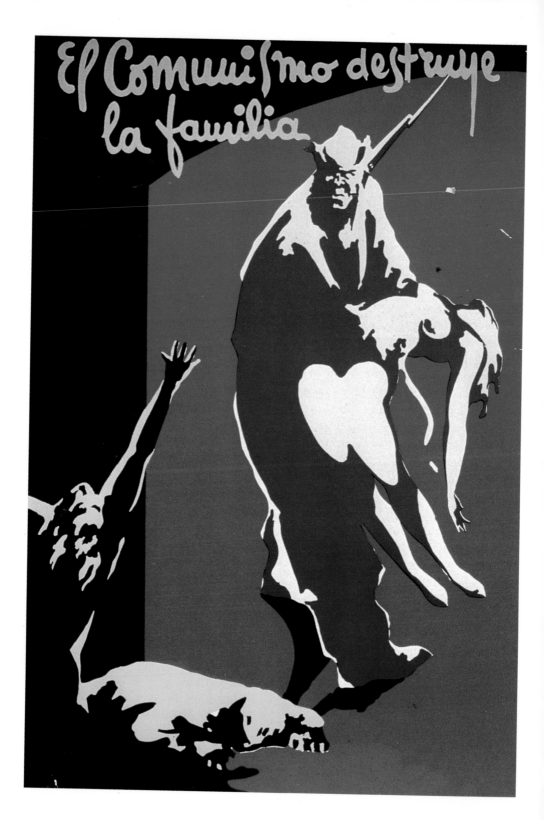

of the fact of death, it is also a thoughtfully conceived image, with the uncanny stare of the dead child returned to the viewer against a patterned rainstorm of aeroplanes. How does *Guernica* match up against the Nationalist poster *Communism Destroys the Family* (FIG. 23)? Crudely sloganed but flamboyantly stylized and coloured, it is modernist in its own way.

One difference between them is that *Guernica* is an original, unique object, while the other images have functioned only as reproductions. This has been an important consideration in distinctions between a "work of art" and a piece of graphic design; it has also often underpinned distinctions between "true art" and "mere propaganda." But a feature of any work of art is that the more it is reproduced photographically and distributed in books, posters, and postcards, the more the original object – the real thing – acquires a special aura. Ever since it was first shown, the possession and location of *Guernica* has been determined by political interests. Picasso started the controversy himself by insisting that the canvas should not be allowed into Spain until the end of Franco's regime (the fascists had won the civil war in 1939). He made the withholding of the object an additional political statement, but one which he could not always control. From 1939 to 1981 it resided in New York's Museum of Modern Art (MoMA), adding greatly to the blue-chip status of the collection and featured there as an episode in the museum's history of modernism. After the death of Franco in 1975 (Picasso had died in 1973) the painting could be "returned" to Spain – but to which part? The town authorities of Guernica wanted it, and so did those of Picasso's birthplace Málaga, and of his childhood village Horta de Sant Juan (formerly Horta de Ebro). Barcelona, which has a Picasso museum among its tourist attractions, also put in a claim. The debate continued for several years. Eventually, in 1981, the Prado got it: "an authentic cultural kidnapping done by the Madrid government," according to the Basque Nationalist Party; a symbol of national reconciliation, according to Prime Minister Adolfo Suárez; and a good photo-opportunity for all the politicians who turned up for its gala reception. The painting was later moved to a special room in Madrid's Museo Nacional Reina Sofía, though postcards of it decorate bars and cafés throughout the Basque region, where it still resonates with separatist sentiment. Overall, the history of *Guernica* shows that the political meaning of any image can never be static or inherent. Nevertheless, as it is known internationally, mainly through photographs, it remains for many people an enduring symbol of resistance to fascism and war.

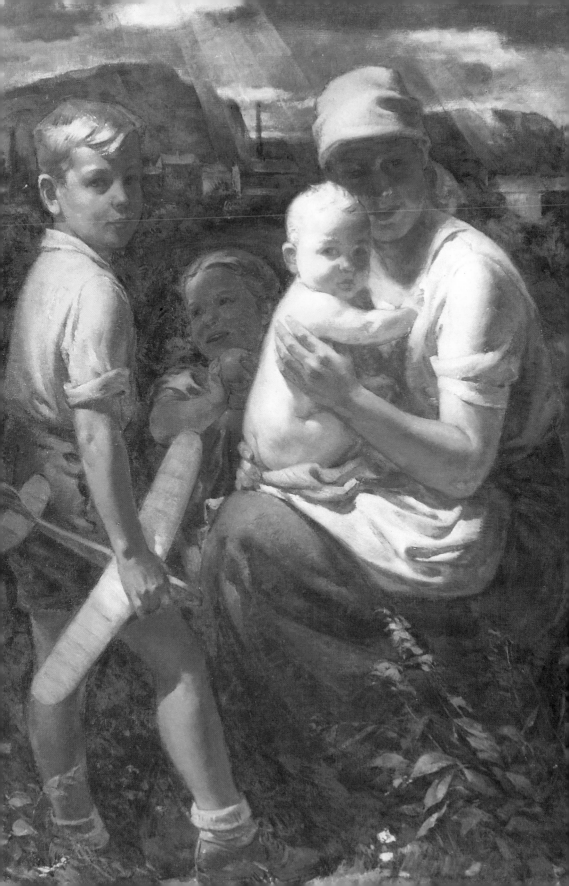

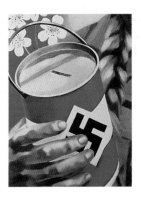

TWO

Art, Propaganda, and Fascism

The term "fascism" does not describe a fixed body of doctrines. Where fascist movements have emerged (in systems of government in Italy, Germany, and Spain, and as a persistent presence in numerous countries, including Britain, France, America, Japan, and South Africa) they have been shaped by local political and cultural traditions. Ideologically, their common factor has been their central claim to combine nationalism with socialism. In practice, the collectivist ideal which this "socialism" implies mainly takes the form of seeking to unite the different classes under a shared sense of allegiance to the common interests of nationality and race. These social bonds are intensified by militarism and fascism's inherent drift towards war.

Fascists emphasized the distinction between their version of socialism and that of communists. One of many key differences between the two ideologies lies in fascism's avowed anti-rationalism. Communist ideologues like Lenin held that communism, despite its emotive rhetoric, is based on scientific objectivity, and that ultimately its ideals appeal to reason. In contrast, fascists openly rejected rationalism as the arid and soulless outlook of bourgeois modernity, and described their movement as a cult of action and passion free of doctrinal rules. Thus the French fascist Robert Brasillach spoke of fascism not as a theory but a "poetry" of faith and emotion, and Mussolini declared: "I am not a statesman, I am more like a mad poet." In the book *Mein Kampf*, which Adolf Hitler wrote while imprisoned in the Landsberg fortress after the failed military coup of 9 November 1923, he stated that a leader could not gain followers by mere explanation or instruction; these have never moved the masses, he argued: "it is always a devotion which has inspired them, and often a kind

24. R. HEYMANN
The German Mother (Die deutsche Mutter), 1942.
Oil on canvas.
Oberfinanzdirektion,
Munich.

of hysteria which has urged them to action." Fascist propaganda seldom promised material comforts, claiming instead to replace the materialism of capitalist life with a realm of spontaneous feeling, physical immediacy, and the reintegration of individuals with the collective soul of their nation.

Fascist propagandists explicitly described this belief as mythic: as a *Weltanschauung* or an all-embracing vision of a spiritually unified and morally regenerated society created by the will of its people as embodied in their leader. German Nazism, distinguished from other fascist variants by its ruthless emphasis on extremist racial theories, construed this new society as a racially pure organic community, or *Volksgemeinschaft*. The appeal of this vision of organic unity was largely due to the crisis in German society which, by 1933 when Hitler seized power, had been traumatized by defeat in the First World War and socially fragmented by the political instability of the Weimar period and by acute economic depression and mass unemployment. Exploiting deep-rooted anti-Semitic traditions, Nazis attributed these disasters to a phase of decadence created by a secret conspiracy of Jews. Promising to replace the confusion and alienation of modern existence with the eternal values of an imagined Aryan culture, the Nazis offered a myth which some historians have called "palingenetic," a form of utopianism which evokes the idea of rebirth or spiritual regeneration. Nazi propaganda did not hesitate to stress that this rebirth, described as a "reconnection forwards," would be generated by a process of destruction.

As with all state propaganda, fascism did not address a single message to a unified audience. The content and methods of its propaganda were diversified in order to target the separate interests of a disparate population. Thus its promise to crush Bolshevism had appeal among the middle classes, while its heroization of manual labour, and the promise of jobs, appealed to working-class audiences. The role of women – though increasingly limited to the spheres of marriage and motherhood – was given a mystical prestige. Schoolchildren were indoctrinated in the classroom and mobilized in their leisure pursuits (FIG. 25). The task

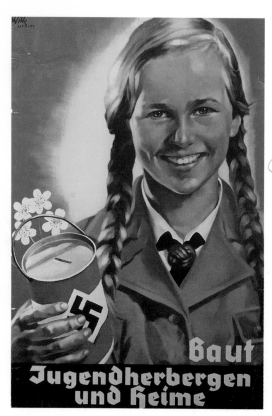

25. HERMANN WITTE
Build Youth Hostels and Homes (Baut Jugendherbergen und Heime), 1938–9. Poster, 33 x 22½" (83.8 x 56.9 cm). Imperial War Museum, London.

for fascist propaganda was to accommodate the values of these disparate constituencies while at the same time conveying the impression of both ideological consistency and national unity. The Nazi or National Socialist German Workers' Party (NSDAP) surpassed the other fascist regimes by achieving this through a highly coordinated and bureaucratically complex propaganda machine. Art functioned as only one component in its programme, but brought to it the legitimizing status of high culture and provided many of the symbols and images of what the Nazis called their "cultural mission."

Fascism and the Aestheticization of Politics

Fascist parties paid close attention to the stylistic "look" of their movement, encompassing the cut and insignia of their uniforms and the new state symbols, like the swastika flag which Hitler claimed to have designed himself. It has often been remarked that fascism's public manifestations took a theatrical and ritualistic form, typified by the numerous parades, ceremonies, and mass rallies. These assembled people in ways designed to give them a sense of group identity and involvement and to make them amenable to emotional manipulation. In Germany a new calendar of national feast days was invented to increase the opportunities for this, and almost every public event was a carefully stage-managed spectacle.

Hitler was fastidious in shaping the style of his public persona. He took lessons from an actor to develop his repertoire of gestures and rhetorical devices, and set up a college for training Party members in public speaking as early as 1928. As part of his leadership cult, or *ducismo*, Mussolini in Italy also developed a code of gestures and highly stylized facial expressions designed to be clearly legible from the back of a crowd. These acting styles may have been borrowed from those of the silent cinema. Hitler and Mussolini clearly sought to emanate an erotic charisma – they both boasted that they could control the crowd "as if it were a woman."

Fascist theatricality was dependent on the technologies of the mass media. In Germany the vast rallies relied on public address systems, and were broadcast on radio and screened in cinemas. Huge architectural spaces were purpose-built, deriving their design from a combination of the sports stadium and the sets of Hollywood musicals. The rallies also borrowed from the earlier theatrical innovations of the Weimar period and in particular from the ideal of the *Gesamtkunstwerk*, or total work of art, in which drama, choreography, music, and architecture are blended together

26. and 27. *Triumph of the Will (Triumph des Willens)*, directed by Leni Riefenstahl, 1934. Film stills.

After the Second World War, Riefenstahl was condemned for her work as a Nazi propagandist. But she insisted that her film of the 1934 Party Congress had not been a propaganda film, but a "documentary." Did Riefenstahl merely film the event as an observer, or was she involved in directing the event itself? Certainly the filming was elaborately planned in advance. Special bridges, towers, and tracking rails were built for high-angle and traveling shots. An aeroplane and airship were made available for the aerial shots, and hand-held cameras were operated from firemen's ladders. The film crew numbered 135 people, including 37 SA and SS men who helped keep order.

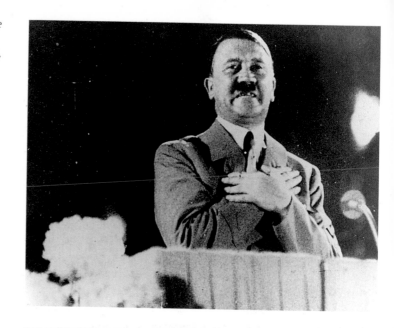

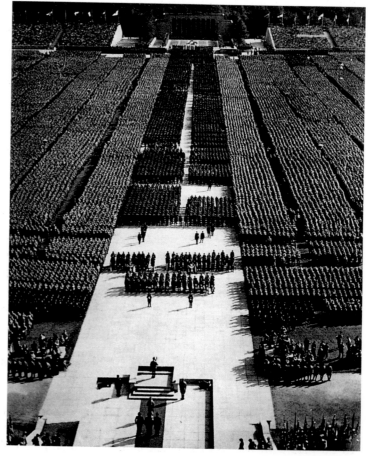

into a total experience. The most famous of these rallies, the Party congress of 1934 – filmed by Leni Riefenstahl as *Triumph of the Will* (FIGS 26 and 27) – shows how the stages of the event were organized into a symbolic pattern of images. In this, the arrangement of people into geometric formations symbolizes the transformation of the formless masses into a united national force. Hitler's procession down a wide aisle between the ranks to rise to his solitary position above them enacts his account of himself as a rank-and-file soldier who had "arisen from the midst of the people" to convey his divine message. His ascension to the viewing stand and the ritual exchange of blessings bears out his public image as both priestly and godlike. Here he is all-seeing and the focus of all eyes. Hitler's claim to be the personification of the will of the people gives a mirror-like structure to this exchange: The people are called upon to see their leader as the reflection of their collective personality. In Riefenstahl's sophisticated film the constant editing between the massed ranks, the swastikas, and Hitler's face expresses the key slogan of the event: "Ein Volk, ein Führer, ein Reich." The rhetoric of Hitler's rally speeches stressed a similar structure of "I, you and us": "And when we [the Party leadership] are no more, your task will be to hold fast to the flag we once raised from the void. And I know that you can and will do no different; for you are flesh of our flesh and blood of our blood; and the spirit that burns in your young minds is the same spirit by which we ourselves are dominated."

As the film shows, the rally took place over several days. Those who took part, mostly young men, travelled together from various parts of the country (the film makes much of this coming together of the regions), and ate, washed, and slept together in military-style camp sites. The level of activities – which continued during the night with speeches, oath-taking, and singing by firelight – indicates the deliberate creation of physical conditions designed to break down the capacity for individual thought or reflection. Lack of privacy, removal from familiar surroundings, and sleep deprivation would have been powerful instruments for engineering emotional vulnerability. These were reinforced by the visual and aural impact of rhythmic repetition over the hours of drilling, drumming, and chanting.

On a local level small-scale rituals often appropriated existing traditions. For example, at Christmas 1933 a nativity play was performed for railway workers. The play took place around a Christmas tree where performers dressed as crusaders acted out the struggle of light against darkness, and Stormtroopers marched to the crib with swastika flags. The commentator announced the symbolic victory: "God sent us a saviour at the moment of our deepest despair: our Führer and our wonderful Stormtroopers." This mixing of politics with religiosity and the fusion of contemporary events with legends of the past were characteristic of Nazism's techniques for achieving a cultic spirit of popular support. In addition, acts of official vandalism – the smashing of shop windows, the burning of books in public – were devised as a kind of macabre street theatre intended to dramatize the division between membership and exclusion.

The theatrical style with which fascism represented its ideology served as the substitute for a democratic constitution. It conferred a sense of popular participation to an entirely authoritarian system. The writer Walter Benjamin (1892-1940), who committed suicide while trying to escape from the Nazi regime in 1940, described fascism as the aestheticization of politics. It does not give the working classes their rights, he wrote, but only the chance to express themselves. Benjamin concluded that with its inner dynamic of permanent revolution, industrial over-production and obsession with death, fascism could only end by consuming itself in warfare. In an alternative interpretation, Albert Speer (1905-81), Hitler's chief architect, recalled in his *Spandau Diaries*: "It was when the ritual was formally agreed upon – indeed it was almost canonized – that I first became aware the whole thing was meant to be taken literally. I had always believed all these parades, processions, and initiation ceremonies to be part of a virtuoso propagandistic review. It was now clear that for Hitler it was a matter of founding a church."

Certainly there were millions of people in Germany who did not agree with Nazi beliefs during the Third Reich, although the possibilities of organized resistance were very limited. The exact proportion of the population that followed National Socialism is not clear, but the Nazi Party did not achieve a genuine electoral majority. Probably only a minority of those who supported Nazism were primarily motivated by anti-Semitism or racism. The photomontages by John Heartfield (1891-1968), which were published in left-wing magazines for the underground and exiled communities, are well-known examples of German anti-fascist culture. *Hurrah, the Butter is All Gone!* (FIG. 28) uses Dadaist satire to expose the absurdity of Nazi rhetoric. Surrounded by swastika wallpaper, a loyal family at the dinner table are eating their bicycle. Grannie chews on a coal shovel and baby sucks an axe. The picture refers to Hermann Göring's remarks on the merits of food shortage; in a speech he had explained: "Iron has always made a country strong, butter and lard only make people fat."

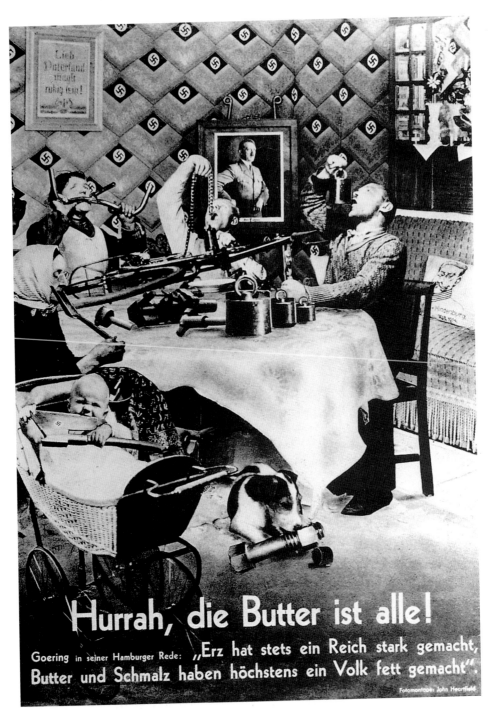

Hurrah, die Butter ist alle!

Goering in seiner Hamburger Rede: „Erz hat stets ein Reich stark gemacht, Butter und Schmalz haben höchstens ein Volk fett gemacht".

Fotomontage: John Heartfield

28. JOHN HEARTFIELD
Hurrah, the Butter is All Gone! (Hurrah, die Butter ist alle!), AIZ, 19 December 1935. Photomontage.

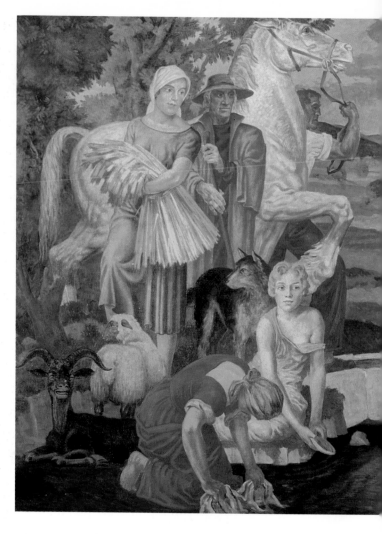

29. GISBERT PALMIÉ
The Rewards of Work, after
1933. Oil on canvas, 4'9" x
9'4" (1.45 x 2.85 cm).
Oberfinanzdirektion,
Munich.

Fascism and Archaism

Fascism rejects the idea of "progress." With its roots in the tradition of the eighteenth-century Enlightenment, the notion of
progress holds that history is shaped in linear fashion by the unfold-
ing of human reason. Fascists would associate this tradition with
liberalism and Marxism (although it also lay in the European colo-
nialist belief in the right to impose "western progress" on "back-
ward" nations). In place of this linear view of history, fascism sees
a circular pattern of rebirth or revival, and envisages a return to
a lost golden age.

    This underlies the prevalence of archaic images and styles in
fascist art and architecture. Fascism did not create any new styles
of art, and none of the regimes used one style exclusively. Under

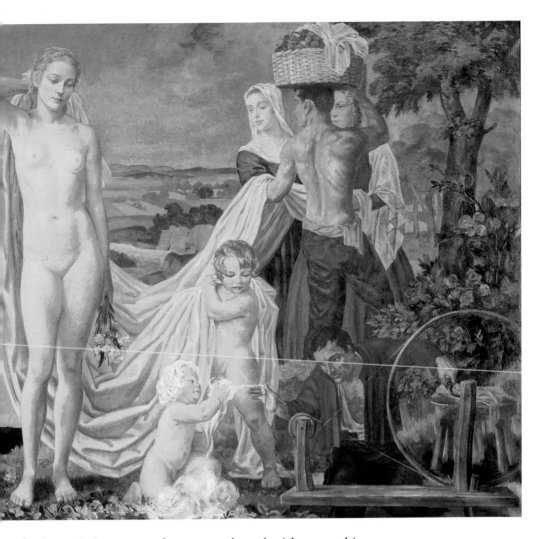

fascism existing types of art were adapted with new subject matter or put in contexts which made them seem political. The criteria for officially favoured art, as refined and regulated by state-sponsored exhibitions, public commissions, and government art magazines, were quite diverse. But a common factor in most fascist art is the evocation of continuity with the past. Thus although fascist paintings may often seem "realistic," fascist aesthetics formally rejected notions of realism which claim merely to reflect the present. Art should instead evoke "eternal values."

In landscape painting, a major genre in the art of the Third Reich (1933–45), the idea of "eternal values" – combining artistic, moral, and social values – is connoted in idyllic images of rural life. *The Rewards of Work* (FIG. 29) portrays the rural community living and working in harmony with the cycles of nature. While

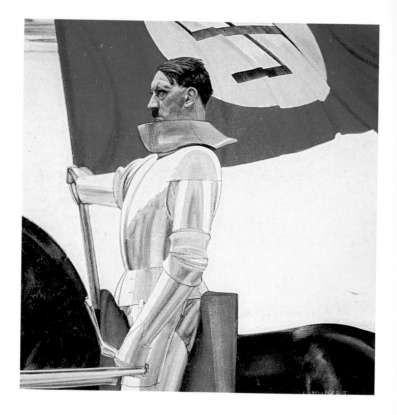

30. HUBERT LANZINGER
The Flag Bearer, after 1933.
US Army Art Collection,
Washington.

Hitler was portrayed as a
crusader who would bring
salvation through warfare.
He had stated: "Humanity
has become what it is
thanks to struggle. ... A
peace that lasts more than
twenty-five years inflicts
great damage on a nation."

agricultural labour was also a common theme in Soviet art, in fascist versions we seldom see the modern tractors of which the Soviet communists were so fond. The Arcadian peasants are using outdated technology and wear costumes of an indeterminate period. Such paintings were made political by their nationalist subtext of "Blood and Soil," a key Nazi slogan and a common title for paintings which show the people rooted to the earth of their homeland and – often through allusions to sowing and reaping – reproducing the genetic purity of their race. Here this idea is conveyed through simple colour symbolism in which the seamless yellow cloth matches the colour of the hair of the main figures: The purest inheritors of the golden age will be blond. The image can be interpreted as both a nostalgic allegory of a lost age and a utopian metaphor for the future world of the new Reich. Its implied political values are naturalized, or made to seem normal and eternal, by their union with the orders of nature.

The Middle Ages are often cited in fascist images with more civic or martial themes. These celebrate an imagined feudal era of unity within a strict social hierarchy. In Italian fascism the medieval iconography of leadership in the figure of the city-state prince was mapped onto the figure of Mussolini, just as Hitler was sometimes

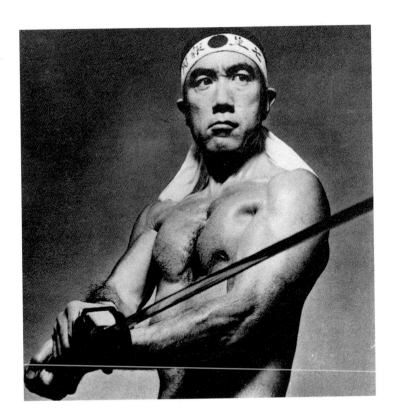

31. KISHIN SHINOYAMA
Yukio Mishima, 1970.
Photograph.

Yukio Mishima, a best-selling writer in Japan, liked to have himself photographed posing as a Samurai warrior. Shortly after this photograph was taken, he committed suicide by ritual disembowelment, an act intended to demonstrate his commitment to the revival of martial and imperialist values. In his auto-biographical writings, Mishima revealed and explored his preoccupation with narcissism and sado-masochism. These seem to have been closely integrated with his emotional adherence to neo-fascism.

portrayed as a Teutonic knight (FIG. 30). Under the Third Reich, medievalism in architecture is seen in the recurrence of vernacular half-timbered buildings held to be more *völkisch* than those of a neo-classical style. Here *völkisch* means "of the people" but carries archaic and racial connotations. For Nazism, medievalism was made problematic by the resistance to the regime of the Catholic Church, and Hitler once described Gothic styles as "too Christian." *Völkisch* imagery, however, often blended Christian traditions with a largely invented paganism. This is seen in the camp-fire and torch-lit rites of Hitler Youth groups and in the occult connotations of the swastika.

In the ultra-nationalist ideology of imperial Japan, religion and politics were fully fused and often expressed in medieval themes. In 1924 the Japanese *Kokuhonsha* organization was founded to propagate the racial supremacy of Japan in the Pacific, and this was expressed in a resurgence of a cult of the Samurai warrior that permeated Japanese militarism. The famous novelist and neo-fascist Yukio Mishima (1925-70) attempted to revive this during the 1960s through his tiny private army, which wore uniforms designed by Mishima and embraced Samurai rituals, martial arts, body-building, and the eroticization of death (FIG. 31). The group advocated

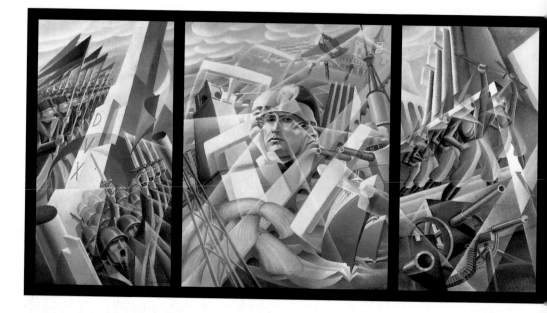

32. ALESSANDRO BRUSCHETTI
Fascist Synthesis , 1935. Oil
on plywood, 5'1" x 9'3"
(1.55 x 2.82 m). The
Mitchell Wolfson Jr.
Collection, Miami Beach,
Florida and Genoa, Italy.

the reinstatement of the political powers of the emperor. Its
attempted coup in 1970 – an entirely theatrical affair involving the
kidnapping of an army general and Mishima's act of *hara-kiri* –
was meticulously prepared for in Mishima's fictional writings and
in his management of the media. Mishima's movement was
small and marginal but was a remarkably pure and self-con-
scious example of fascism as the aestheticization of politics.

Fascist archaism conceals a contradictory attitude towards
modernity. For, while the regimes claimed to restore values that
preceded modern decadence, they also instigated intensive industrialization to build up their economic and military bases. The use
of neo-classicism as a monumental style for large public buildings
in Italy and Germany partly served to resolve this paradox. Applied
to factories, railway stations, and motorways, it conveyed an air
of stability and Apollonian grandeur. But this was a very stream-
lined version of classicism, often only a thin façade that concealed
a structure of modernist functionalism. By no means exclusive
to fascism, this style was widely employed throughout Europe and
the United States in the 1920s and 1930s, and prolifically by Stalin.
For both fascism and Stalinism it was an effective way of expressing cultural conservatism in a modern setting. In addition, both
Hitler and Mussolini exploited its overtones of Roman Imperialism to pose as the new emperors of Europe.

Under Mussolini's regime in Italy propaganda and censorship
were widespread, and the Italian fascists regarded their movement
as the vanguard of an artistic renaissance. However, the govern-

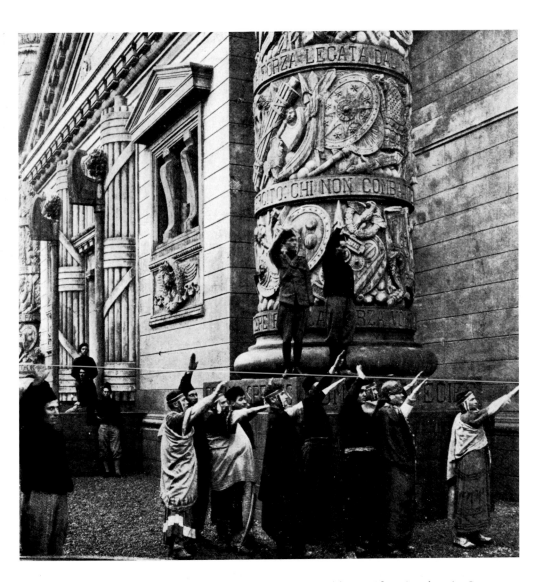

33. Historical pageant marking the inauguration of a Casa del Fascio in Tuscany, c. 1928.

The building's neo-Imperial facade incorporates a pair of giant *fasces*, the bound bundle of rods that symbolized the authority of ancient Román magistrates and from which the word fascism was derived.

ment's cultural policy imposed less uniformity than in Germany. Fascist art could be overtly modernist, as in the futuristic painting *Fascist Synthesis* (FIG. 32) by Alessandro Bruschetti (1910–81). As the title implies, the painting depicts a fascist universe in which the old and the new are brought together in dynamic synthesis. Ancient buildings and electricity pylons, swords and machine-guns coexist, and are activated in a kind of regimented frenzy presided over by the spirit of Mussolini (FIG. 33). His face appears in the centre, shown as a multiple image which recalls the effects of cinematic montage. A similar effect is used in *Continuous Profile of Mussolini* of 1933 (FIG. 34) by Renato Bertelli (1900–74). Mussolini's features, as unmistakable as a corporate logo, are reproduced through

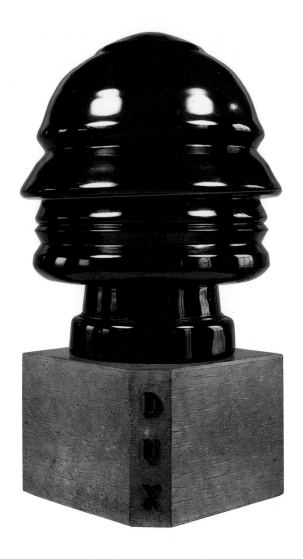

34. Renato Bertelli
*Continuous Profile of
Mussolini*, 1933. Ceramic,
height 11³/₄" (29.8 cm),
diameter 9" (22.8 cm).
Imperial War Museum,
London.

360 degrees. The sculpture implies that the leader's vision, and the power of his government extend in all directions from a fixed centre.

The supposedly eternal values of high culture have been used throughout history to legitimize power and privilege. But this function is made more complex under regimes, fascist or communist, which purport to be movements of the masses. In exploiting the high-class status of traditional art, their propagandists risk alienating working-class audiences for whom an oil painting in a museum may be viewed as an inherently hostile object in an elitist environment. The regimes sought to counter this effect by merging fine art with mass culture. This used two related strategies: first, the mass-reproduction of paintings and sculptures in films, posters, postcards, advertisements, and magazines, which shift the sites of reception and confer a sense of common ownership over the image; and second, by the stylistic adaptation of art to the visual codes of popular culture – by making a painting look like a movie poster or a pornographic pin-up, for example. The results have often been termed "kitsch," a term that refers to art specifically styled for mass consumption. Of course, the regimes could simultaneously use high culture on a monumental scale to intimidate and belittle people.

"Coordination" (*Gleichschaltung*) was the euphemism which Nazis used to describe the enforcement of political conformity. In the press and publishing industries, the education system, and in all art institutions, politically suspect or "racially impure" people were sacked. As a Party spokesman stated in 1934, the aim of Nazism was to be "a total ordering of the German people," which must "above all be uniform, born from a single spirit, and extended from a single central point systematically over the entire social life." As in Stalin's imposition of Soviet orthodoxy in the field of art, which also took place in the early 1930s, the Nazi regime abolished independent art groups and replaced them with a single organization integrated with the state. This was the National Chamber of Culture (*Reichskulturkammer*) founded in autumn 1933 under Josef Goebbels, Minister for People's Enlightenment and Propaganda. This organization consisted of seven chambers, for music, the visual arts, literature, theatre, the press, radio, and film. Each chamber was in turn divided into subsections; the chamber for visual arts included departments for painting, sculpture, architecture, interior and graphic design, craft associations, art publishing, sales, and auctioneering. As stated in the law which established the National Chamber of Culture, its purpose was to "merge together the creative elements from all fields for carrying out, under the leadership of the state, a single will." Only racially and ideologically acceptable artists were admitted to the chamber. Although many artists left Germany at this time, or remained in "internal exile," approximately 100,000 practitioners had joined the National Chamber of Culture by 1935, including 15,000 architects, 14,300 painters, 2,900 sculptors, and 6,000 designers.

Nazism and the Avant-Garde

In view of the cultural conservatism of the National Socialist Party, it might be assumed that the Nazis were entirely antagonistic towards avant-garde art and banned it from the outset. But recent

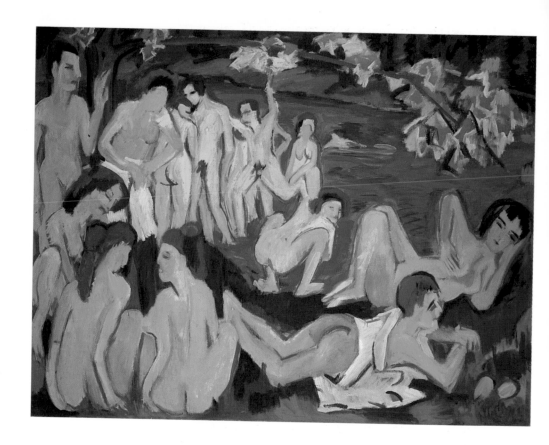

35. ERNST LUDWIG KIRCHNER
Bathers at Moritzburg,
1909–26. Oil on canvas,
4'11¾" x 3'11¼" (1.51 x
1.20 m). Tate Gallery,
London.

art-historical studies reveal a more ambiguous relationship. It is true that by 1937 the Nazi leadership made clear its rejection of modernist art, and avant-garde artists were excluded and thoroughly persecuted. But this was preceded by some years of debate among senior Party officials. Josef Goebbels argued that some artists of the German Expressionist movement, such as Emil Nolde (1867-1956), Erich Heckel (1883-1970), Ernst Ludwig Kirchner (1880-1938), Karl Schmidt-Rottluff (1884-1976), and Ernst Barlach (1870-1938) represented a national spirit in German art which could be embraced by the Third Reich. This is surprising at first sight, for the artists themselves could not be described as Nazi followers, although Nolde had briefly joined the Party. Their brand of Expressionism was anti-authoritarian and individualistic. Yet within their politically muddled outlook, Goebbels may well have perceived some affinities with the Nazi *Weltanschauung.* A selective reading of Expressionist writings finds some fiercely nationalistic declarations and a vague anti-capitalism which opposes the cosmopolitan sophistication of urban society and contrasts this with nostalgic images of a community spiritually unified and at one with nature

(FIG. 35). In addition, the Expressionists' art and lifestyle proclaimed the precedence of physical sensations and passion over the intellect, a sentiment shared with Nazism's cult of action. On racialist grounds, Nazis deplored the Expressionists' use of styles from African art, which was entirely at variance with their standards of "Aryan beauty." And yet the Expressionists' romantic view of so-called "primitive" life finds a distant echo in Nazism's primitivist celebration of *völkische* culture.

It would be wrong to describe Expressionism as proto-Nazi, and to understate the persecution which the artists later suffered. It would be more accurate to say that as separate discourses, Expressionism and National Socialism were both shaped by a strong inclination in German culture which sought anti-rationalist alternatives to the alienation and social fragmentation of bourgeois capitalism. There had been a widespread "back to nature" trend in Germany since the turn of the century, which was manifested in the camping and hiking youth movements and in a thriving vogue for nudism during the 1920s. Many youth groups and nudist clubs were linked with left-wing organizations. The Nazis banned them, but appropriated and exploited some of the sentiments that informed them.

Despite Goebbels' support, Expressionism had often been publicly attacked by senior Nazis, including Hitler and Alfred Rosenberg, and modernist art and its supporters began to be purged from museums shortly after Hitler seized power. For those in the mainstream, modern art was a conspicuous target through which the Party could intimidate non-Nazi intellectuals and demonstrate its power to enforce conformity. And, importantly, the attack on Expressionism could be used to articulate National Socialism's theory of "degeneracy," a major theme in its ideology. This was put across in a typically lurid and theatrical manner in the exhibition *Degenerate Art* (*Entartete Kunst*) which opened in Munich in July 1937 (FIGS 36 and 37).

The *Degenerate Art* exhibition displayed more than 700 works of modernist art solely for the purpose of mocking and vilifying them. Many of the exhibits had been confiscated from public collections and represented more than a hundred artists across the range of modernism. The paintings were hung erratically, often unframed, alongside labels giving the price that the public museums had paid for them and statements by modernist critics and artists written on the walls. These were accompanied by sarcastic captions written by Hitler, and by large slogans which denounced the art's obscenity, insanity, blasphemy, and "Niggerization" (*Verniggerung*), which referred to the stylistic derivations of African

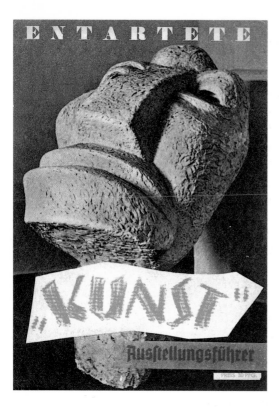

36. *Degenerate Art* exhibition catalogue, 1937, showing Otto Freundlich's sculpture *The New Man*. Freundlich (1878-1943) died in a concentration camp.

37. Josef Goebbels visiting the *Degenerate Art* Exhibition, 1937.

The exhibition was conceived as a kind of show trial. Visitors were encouraged to scoff at the "degenerate" avant-garde art on display. During the four months it was on view in Munich it was said to have been visited by more than two million people. It subsequently toured thirteen German and Austrian cities where it was seen by nearly a further million. It has been described as the most widely attended art exhibition ever. What most of the visitors really thought of the avant-garde art on show remains unknown.

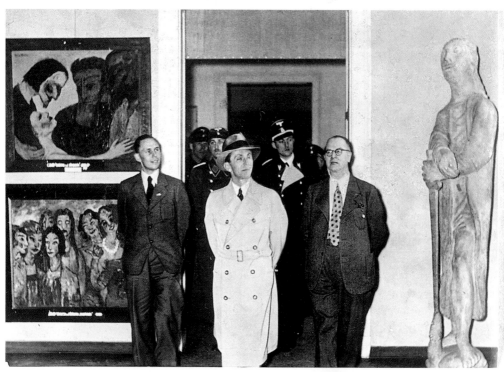

art. Overall the exhibits were denounced as "Cultural Bolshevism" (*Kultur-Bolschewismus*) and attributed to a conspiracy of "Jewish Imperialism."

As a key idea in Nazi theory, "degeneracy" derived from nineteenth-century medical terminology used to describe genetic deformity. The writer Max Nordau, author of *Degeneration* (*Entartung*, 1893), was the first to popularize the use of the term to define the overall decay of civilization. This was characteristic of a *fin de siècle* reaction against the conditions of modern urban life which perceived their effects in pathological terms (similar theories elsewhere in Europe evoked "neurasthenia," or nervous exhaustion). Degeneracy implied weakness and disorder and readily merged with political metaphors that used the language of sickness and infection to describe political and racial impurity. In a speech on art made at the time of the exhibition, Hitler employed a similar blend of literal and metaphorical allusions to sickness by arguing that the distortions in modernist art were symptomatic either of the actual degeneration of the artists' mental and perceptual faculties, or of their aim to deceive and pervert the nation. In either case, the potential penalties were made clear in Hitler's open reference to the Nazi practice of killing political enemies and mentally and physically handicapped people. In the same year, the Ministry for Education and Science published a pamphlet which stated that modern art was "the strongest proof of the necessity of a radical solution of the Jewish question."

Throughout Europe and the United States at this time widespread attacks on modern art by conservative critics also linked it with Jewishness, Bolshevism, madness, and homosexuality. But under fascist regimes, this discourse of degeneracy had the special function of amplifying their claims to be creating a cleansed and reborn social order. Much fascist propaganda played on dichotomies of darkness and light, decay and renewal, death and rebirth. Accordingly, the *Degenerate Art* exhibition, when it opened in Munich, was twinned with a larger exhibition called the *Great German Art Exhibition* (*Grosse Deutsche Kunstausstellung*) which opened nearby and took place annually from 1937 until 1944. This show of new art favoured by the regime inaugurated the vast new House of German Art (*Haus der Deutschen Kunst*), one of the Third Reich's first major public building projects. Its opening was accompanied by a huge procession of floats and followers in historic costumes, embodying the renaissance of national culture. Similar Day of German Art Festivals were repeated annually. The event in 1939 was recorded in colour by members of Munich's Amateur Film Society (FIG. 38).

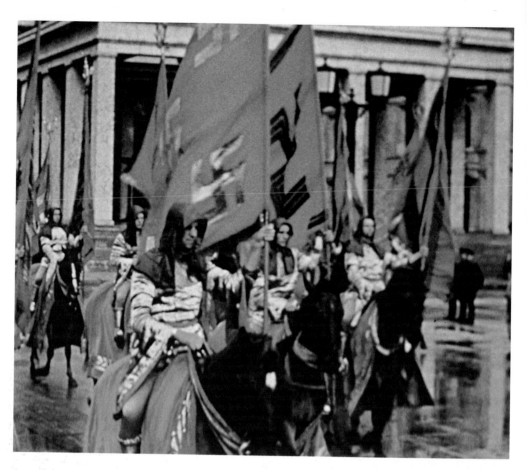

38. The Day of German Art Festival, Munich, 14 July, 1939. Film still, 16mm Kodachrome.

Fascist Interpretations of the Body

In Nazism, the treatment of the body, in both art and real life, articulated doctrines of racist theory, beliefs about the respective roles of men and women, and concepts of the organic unity of the nation-state. Ideals of bodily beauty provide the premise of Ivo Saliger's painting *The Judgement of Paris* (FIG. 39), which adopts a subject that has recurred throughout centuries of Western art. The mortal Paris is called on to assess the naked bodies of three goddesses and to reward the most beautiful with a golden apple. Historically, this subject had allowed artists to show off their ability to handle the ideal female form, and to complement the physical beauty of the bodies depicted with the artistic beauty and skill of the painting. In this instance, the pale, classically-proportioned bodies, and the style of the work, which would have passed as neoclassical or "Hellenic," would both have been deemed "Aryan." The painting therefore related to Nazi theories which identified various qualities of Aryan superiority, the Aryan race being deemed the most lucid, spiritual, creative, and so forth. Among these qualities, the Aryans' supposedly superior physical beauty was held to be the ultimate evidence of natural supremacy. These beliefs motivated the policies of scrutiny to which millions of individuals were subjected. The bureaucratic examination of family backgrounds in search of Jewish lineage, the medical diagnosis of physical or mental disability, and police evidence of homosexuality were all used to label people as enemies of the master race. In addition to systematically killing such people, programmes of Nazi eugenics, which instigated selective breeding and sterilization, aimed to purify the genetic make-up of the population of the future. Among the means available for this, a law was passed in December 1933 whereby the minimum age for "voluntary" sterilization was set at ten, and compulsory sterilization at fourteen. 110,000 adults and children had been sterilized by the end of 1935, and thousands more were killed in "medical" institutions. Under these circumstances, and within the specific framework of Nazi ideology, works of art which intentionally promoted the concept of Aryan beauty

39. IVO SALIGER
The Judgement of Paris,
1939. Oil on canvas, 5'2" x 6'7" (1.6 x 2 m).

In a speech in 1937, Hitler proclaimed: "Never was mankind closer than now to Antiquity in its appearance and its sensibilities. Sport contests and competitions are hardening millions of youthful bodies, displaying them to us more and more in a form and temper that they have neither manifested nor been thought to possess for perhaps a thousand years." Hitler's notion of physical beauty referred specifically to Aryan "racial purity."

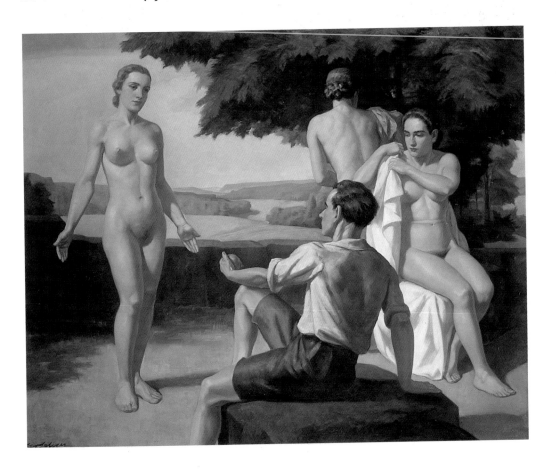

and excluded "ugliness" and "impurity" were actively complicit with the practice of excluding and ultimately exterminating non-Aryan people – principally Jews, and the "Slavic races" of Eastern Europe and the Soviet Union. From within this evil and peculiarly aesthetic perspective, the campaign of genocide against Jews and the killing of approximately 20 million Soviet people during the Second World War were perceived as "cultural achievements."

The 1936 Berlin Olympic Games provided a conspicuous opportunity for the regime to adapt its mass-rally mode of political spectacle for consumption by international audiences. As a contest of physical excellence, aggrandized by the pseudo-Hellenic ethos of the Olympic tradition, the event was an ideal vehicle for insinuating Nazi mythology into the popular culture of sport. Leni Riefenstahl was commissioned to record the games for the cinema, and her resulting film, *Olympia*, released in two parts, *Festival of the Nations* (*Fest der Völker*) and *Festival of Beauty* (*Fest der Schönheit*), testifies to the Nazi cult of physical beauty and power (FIGS 40 and 41). Like *Triumph of the Will*, her film is not an objective documentary. The coverage of the sporting competitions is preceded by an opening sequence which shows the origins of the Olympic spirit in ancient Greece. Nude male and female "Greek" athletes, who emerge like classical statues from an archaic landscape, generate the Olympic flame, which is mystically transported through time and space from the mountains of ancient Greece to the Berlin stadium. This is the allegory of the westward march and ascendancy of Aryan culture. It is characteristic of the National Socialist tendency to mythologize history by veiling the present (the unsettling and banal flux of everyday modern life) behind vistas of the distant past and intimations of heroic destiny in the future.

By featuring female athletes, Riefenstahl makes a relatively positive representation of women as active achievers, albeit in a role separated from the world of work. This imagery contrasts with the bland pornography so prevalent in Nazi art; erotic nudes featured heavily in the art purchases of senior Party men. The contrast relates to a wider internal conflict within Nazi values, in which there was some contradiction between the neurotic misogyny often found in its rhetoric, and the presence within the movement of many women activists. National Socialist women's magazines like *Women's Watch* (*Frauen Warte*) and *The German Woman Fighter* (*Die Deutsche Kämpferin*) had sometimes depicted positive role models for women, like that of the Nordic female warrior or the modern career woman – like Riefenstahl herself.

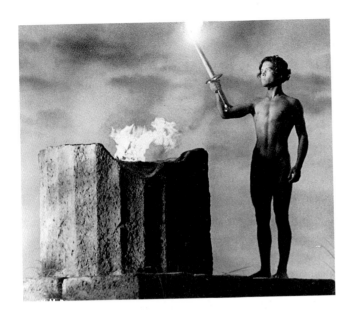

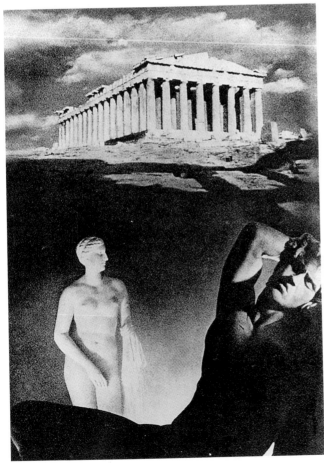

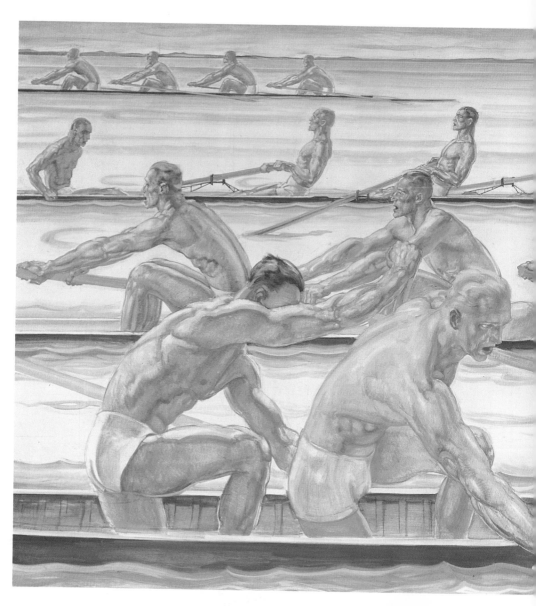

42. ALBERT JANESCH
Water Sport (Wassersport),
1936. Oil on canvas, 5' x
6'11" (1.53 x 2.08 m).
Oberfinanzdirektion,
Munich.

Party ideology aimed to reconcile the contradictory messages about the strength of the German woman and her natural subservience by channelling notions of strength and service back to the domestic sphere and child-bearing. Child-bearing was explicitly cast as the means to propagate the nation and to provide the future manpower required for warfare and labour. The subtext of the many paintings of motherhood exhibited in official sites during the Third Reich was the spiritual elevation of maternity, in which female strength was to be measured by the willing sacrifice of children to war (see FIG. 24).

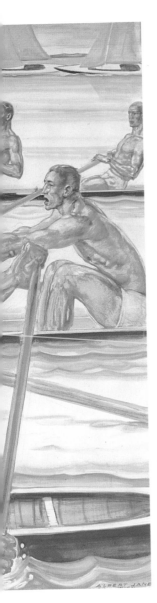

Fascist interpretations of the human body supported an overarching metaphor which viewed the body as a model for the state. Like parts of a body, each part of the state should operate in harmony, but not in equality: As the head has power over the limbs, so the government has power over the people. But government and people are organically bonded together and thus the state is fused with the nation. The body of the state is pure, purged of internal diseases and immune to external contaminations. Although this concept of organic unity has featured over the centuries in Western political thought, it had a particular importance for fascism. The centrality of this metaphor is relevant to almost every representation of the human body in fascist art. Images of bodily strength, vigour, aggression, and alertness, such as Albert Janesch's *Water Sport* (FIG. 42) and Adolf Wamper's *Genius of Victory* (FIG. 43), all reflected on the intended qualities of the fascist state.

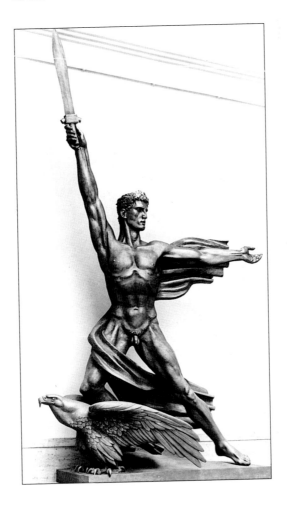

43. ADOLF WAMPER
Genius of Victory, 1940.

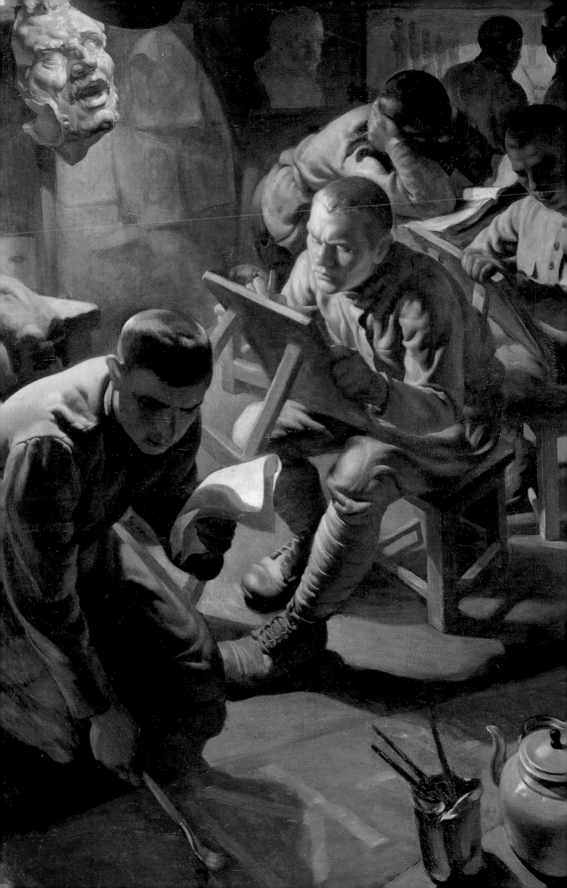

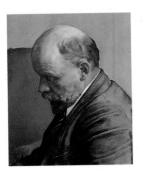

THREE

Propaganda in the Communist State

I n theory, communism views revolution as a continuous process which transforms consciousness alongside the transformation of social reality. As implemented by state communism, national programmes of reconstruction, like industrialization or the collectivization of agriculture, were intended to have profound effects on people's habits of thought and behaviour, to an extent that would far exceed the mere propaganda of words and images. In practice, communist regimes have represented social change through a screen of censorship and illusion, producing a condition which some have described as dream-like because the official version of reality is so far at odds with everyday life. For the long-lasting regimes, like that of the Soviet Union, the term "propaganda" has not had negative connotations among communists, and because communism is said to provide an objective and scientific understanding of the world, little distinction is made between propaganda and education. In art, the main expression of state communism has been Socialist Realism, formally defined and introduced under Joseph Stalin in 1934 as the official aesthetic of the Soviet Union and later imposed by communist states throughout the world. It has been one of the most widely practised and enduring artistic approaches of the twentieth century.

It has often been argued that Socialist Realism was essentially similar to the official art of Nazi Germany. There are certainly many points of comparison. Both emerged fully in the 1930s and produced images which idealized workers and peasants and elevated their leaders in personality cults. Both used easily readable populist styles. The Soviet and Nazi regimes both backed up the persuasive techniques of propaganda with brutal methods of coercion which included arbitrary imprisonment and mass-murder. But

44. SERAFIMA RYANGINA
Red Army Art Studio, 1928.
Oil on canvas, 5'11" x 4'2"
(1.55 x 1.33 m). Central
Red Army Museum,
Moscow.

a closer look at the iconographies of the two systems reveals important differences. Ideologically, communism and fascism took very different views of nature, technology, work, warfare, history, and human purpose. These ideological distinctions were moulded by deeply rooted cultural and social traditions specific to each national context. A conspicuous contrast, as noted earlier, was between Nazism's mythic glorification of the past and Soviet communism's enthusiasm for progress. Nazism emerged partly as a reaction against the instability produced by Germany's rapid modernization. In the Soviet Union, however, as in other communist nations such as the People's Republic of China, Cuba, and the Afro-Marxist states in post-colonial Africa, political revolution took place in advance of substantial modernization. The achievement of modernity was an aspiration closely linked to the establishment of communist society.

"Organizing the Psyche of the Masses"

The imposition of Socialist Realism in 1934 marked a substantial increase in the Soviet state's control over art and was characteristic of Stalin's rule over the Party, exercised since the late 1920s. But it was preceded during the years which followed the October Revolution of 1917 by a period when the leadership had allowed and encouraged the experiments of many different communist art groups and the heated debates between them. These debates were not only about the most suitable style for communist art, but concerned wider questions about the function of art in this new society. From the outset it was clear that the revolution which created the world's first Workers' and Peasants' Government had entirely altered conditions for the patronage, audience, and sites of art. Soviet art was to be principally state-funded, public, and directed to a mass audience. But how were "the masses" to be conceived? What was to be their role in the production of art; what was the status of their tastes; and what was art supposed to *do* to them? These issues provoked a cluster of further questions: Should culture become "proletarian," or should it just be called "socialist" and aspire to be classless? Should it incorporate the achievements of bourgeois culture, or were all traditional kinds of art irredeemably tainted with capitalism and therefore to be abandoned?

Black Square by Kazimir Malevich (1878-1935; FIG. 45) encapsulates a radical view of this unique situation. It consists only of a black square on a white background. Painted shortly before the revolution and exhibited in 1915, Malevich originally conceived

45. KAZIMIR MALEVICH
Black Square, 1914–15. Oil on canvas, 31³/₁₆ x 31⁵/₁₆" (79.2 x 79.5 cm). Tretyakov Gallery, Moscow.

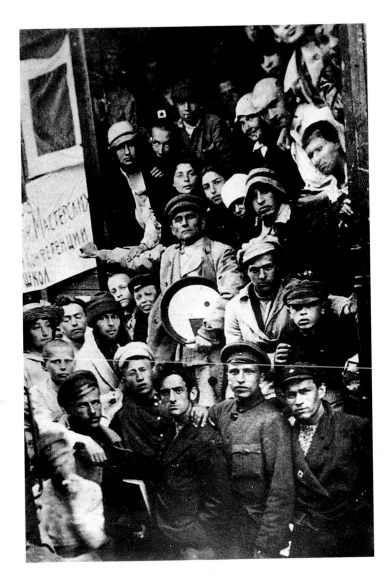

46. Kazimir Malevich and members of UNOVIS en route from Vitebsk to the first All-Russian Conference of Teachers and Students of Art in Moscow, 1920.

it as an extremist avant-garde gesture which announced the end of tradition in painting and the beginning of a transcendental, or what he called "Suprematist," level of perception and representation. He declared: "I have transformed myself into the zero of form and dragged myself out of the rubbish-filled pool of Academic art." The meanings of the painting were altered by the new context of the October Revolution of 1917. From that date, he used it to symbolize a rupture in history, the termination of the old order and the birth of the future out of revolution. For Malevich and his followers in the group UNOVIS (Affirmers of the New Art, FIG. 46), old-fashioned approaches to art could only confine the human mind to conservative ways of thinking. Against this, they developed abstract art in which a vocabulary of pure geometric forms, usually brightly coloured, were designed to address the viewer's senses with dynamic effect. The Russian avant-garde had described this effect as *sdvig* – a sudden enlightenment or "shift" of perception. Though he called them "non-objective," meaning abstract, some of Malevich's paintings refer in their titles and appearance to a cosmic or interplanetary environment signifying the transcendence of earth-bound habits of thought and the creation of a new world. Malevich's ideas drew on Apocalyptic beliefs that had long been nurtured in Russian culture, predicting the revelation of God's will to humanity along with the end of the material world and the creation of a celestial realm of pure spirit. A feature of this belief is the idea that divine knowledge will be revealed in abstract form, unmediated by language. Beyond the partial revelations of the Old and New Testaments, a "Third Text" will communicate directly to the human soul. Malevich saw this as a model for the imminent illumination of the consciousness of the proletariat.

The Bolsheviks' leader, Lenin, more pragmatic and suspicious of avant-garde extremes, viewed the function of art as lying within the broader framework of education, for which tackling the illiteracy of 80 per cent of the population and the scarcity of basic technical skills were the real priorities. Conservative in taste, he felt that socialist culture should build on the best achievements of the past and, by developing these, "raise" the cultural standards of the masses. This was linked to his view of the role of the Party, the main theoretical element of Marxism-Leninism. To Lenin, the Russian working classes, mainly rural peasants, were not ready to generate revolutionary consciousness by themselves. The outbreak of strikes and rioting in cities in the winter of 1916-17, which forced the abdication of the Tsar, had been what Lenin called with some disdain "spontaneous": a premature, disorganized rebellion uninformed by political awareness. Lenin himself, like many other Bolsheviks, was in exile at the time and had to return to Russia to take charge of the uprising and oust the weak provisional government in the *coup* of October. The Party was to provide leadership and formulate the theoretical basis of policy. As in *Lenin at Smolnyi* (FIG. 47) by Isaak Brodsky (1884-1939), which was painted six years after Lenin's death, many paintings of Lenin show him writing or holding a book; these validate his self-appointed position as the legitimate interpreter of doctrine.

The October Revolution was followed by almost four years of civil war, which saw an emphasis on "agitational propaganda"

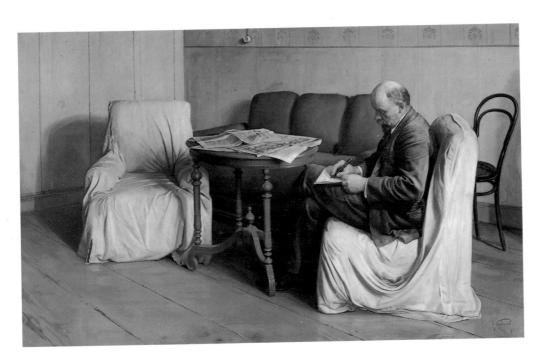

47. Isaak Brodsky
Lenin at Smolnyi, 1930. Oil
on canvas, 6'2¾" x 9'5"
(1.9 x 2.87 m). Tretyakov
Gallery, Moscow.

or agit-prop, a term that described the more immediate, emotional techniques of propaganda. Of early agit-prop practices, street festivals and mass-action dramas revealed a version of public art which stressed popular involvement. Aiming to maintain the momentum of revolutionary enthusiasm in the face of the hardships of the civil war, agit-prop groups sought to create an atmosphere of colourful celebration. Alongside the posters, murals, and huge decorations on buildings, elaborate floats using trucks, trams, or horse-drawn carts carried tableaux of revolutionary themes. Derived partly from festivals of the French Revolution, they also combined the tradition of Russian Orthodox ceremonial processions with the carnivalesque styles of folk entertainment, incorporating clowns, life-size puppets, street criers, and circus acrobats as well as the ballet of the Bolshoi Theatre. The third anniversary of the October Revolution was celebrated by a reenactment of the storming of the Winter Palace performed by a cast of thousands mobilized by the drama groups of the Red Army and Navy. Outside the palace a stage had been built with two platforms, a red one for the workers and a white one for the aristocrats (FIG. 48). A battle was fought out on a bridge between them. The aristocrats were routed and fled in trucks pursued by military searchlight beams and accompanied by artillery salvoes and a volley fired from the *Aurora* battleship anchored nearby on the River Neva. Inside the palace, with what the director called a "cinematic effect," each

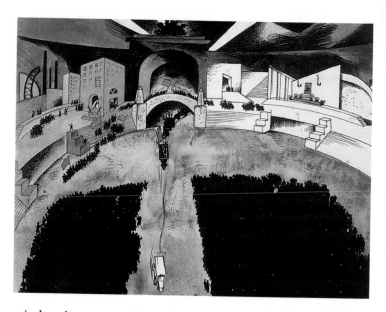

48. YURI ANNENKOV
Design sketch for the
reenactment of the storming
of the Winter Palace, 1920.
Pencil, indian ink, and
watercolour on paper.

window in turn was lit up by a spotlight to reveal a sequence
of fighting scenes. Victory was announced by a firework display on the roof while a massed band played the *Internationale*.

The dramatic reinvention of the revolution as carnival related
to a vein in Marxism which envisages the future as a condition
in which all human activities, harmonized by collective endeavour, become playful or creative. By the late 1930s, this ludic spirit
would begin to decay into the dour and ominous parades of marching athletes and military hardware that characterized Stalin's state
rituals and that would increasingly resemble the morbid ceremonies
of Nazi Germany. But in its earliest years, under the slogan "the
theatricalization of life," mass drama, devised by artists more than
politicians, sought to dissolve distinctions between actors and spec-
tators, and between the production and reception of propaganda.
This presaged later Nazi methods of mass-participation in propaganda events, but the Soviet version was motivated by more
egalitarian values. The implied ideal of ending artistic profes-
sionalism and beginning a culture of universal creativity was close
to the spirit of the network of proletarian culture organizations
called the *proletkults*. Founded in 1917, the *proletkults* were a movement of utopian adult education, seeking to generate collective
working-class culture from the roots. By the end of 1918 the movement was said to have some 400,000 members, 1,000 training
studios and cells in every major factory. Its leading theorist, Aleksandr Bogdanov (1873-1928), was a philosopher, science fiction
novelist and maverick Party member who believed with mystical fervour in the supernatural powers ready to be set free by

the collectivization of the working classes and the harnessing of their creative potential. Bogdanov also insisted that art develops independently of economic and political spheres, and sought the autonomy of the *proletkults* from Party control. To Lenin, however, this amounted to a challenge to the Party's authority and in 1920 he moved against the organization, limiting its powers and bringing it under Party jurisdiction. Bogdanov was forced out of the *proletkults* and turned his attention to medical experiments. He was fascinated by the potential of blood transfusions, which embodied his faith in science and human regeneration. As if confirming his belief in the sacrifice of the individual for humanity's future, he died in 1928 while experimenting on himself.

Lenin acknowledged the value of the mass dramas, but wanted a more dignified statement of Bolshevism's cultural standards. His own contribution to this was known as the plan for monumental propaganda, which he announced in April 1918 in *Pravda* under a headline which called for "The Removal of Monuments Erected in Honour of the Tsars and their Servants and the Production of Projects for Monuments to the Russian Socialist Revolution." Lenin proposed putting the unemployed to work in pulling down Tsarist statues and replacing them with new monuments commissioned to celebrate revered figures of the past. A list of more than sixty of these was to include historic revolutionaries such as Marx, Engels, Robespierre, and Spartacus, as well as cultural figures such as Tolstoy, Dostoevsky, Rublev, Chopin, and Byron. The statues, in bust or full-length, were hastily knocked up in temporary materials like wood and plaster, and formally unveiled in numerous town squares and on street corners.

Lenin's plan was designed to convey a number of messages about his own views on the role of art. Its ethos was educational – each statue bore a plaque with a brief biography and history lesson – and in contrast with Bogdanov's grass-roots proletarianism, Lenin's was an exercise in sober didacticism aimed at elevating the popular taste. The inclusion of politically conservative writers and artists may also have been intended to reassure the non-communist bourgeoisie about the Party's aesthetic tolerance and respect for Russian heritage. Lenin was sensitive about the reputation of Bolshevism in the West, where the press often depicted it as a movement of barbarous criminality (FIG. 49). He did not prescribe the style that the statues should take; sculptors were given a free hand and thus the programme also served as a forum for discussion about the virtues of different styles. This relative freedom and the modest scale of the statues contrasts with the later conformity of Stalinist monumentalism, though Lenin's

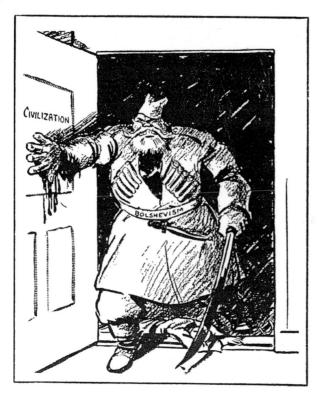

plan would be cited as a precedent for the monstrous statues of political leaders that became *de rigueur* under communist regimes, and that looked down on their citizens as eerie reminders of the omnipresence of state power and surveillance.

Russian avant-garde groups had a troubled relationship with the Party leadership. But in the early years, though small in number, they were well organized, highly energetic, and included some of the relatively few artists who supported Bolshevism. This won them powerful positions in the early Soviet arts administration. Vladimir Tatlin (1885-1953) had been the head of the Moscow branch of *IZO Narkompros* (the Commissariat of Enlightenment's Department of Fine Arts) shortly before conceiving his plans for his famous *Model of the Monument to the Third International* completed in 1920 (FIG. 50). As an abstract alternative to Lenin's figurative monuments, Tatlin's tower was a model for what would be the tallest building in the world. Suspended inside its skeletal framework, a series of glass buildings was planned to accommodate the government of the future. Like parts in a machine, the buildings would slowly revolve, keeping pace with the movement of the planets. Study of Tatlin's design has revealed layers of esoteric symbolism incorporating astrological and alchemical codes. But the tower was also to act as a centre for mass communication. It would be crowned by a radio station and the whole structure would serve as transmitter of propaganda. Information from around the world would be collected by radio receivers and a telephone and telegraph exchange. The agitation centre would broadcast appeals and proclamations to the city. In the evenings the monument would become a giant outdoor cinema, showing newsreels on a screen hung from the building's wings and, in response to current events, appropriate slogans would be written across the skies from a projector station in letters of light. Manifestly impossible to realize at the time, the model acted as an icon for the future accomplishments of Soviet modernization.

49. *On the Threshold,* cartoon, *Los Angeles Times,* 1920.

Anti-Bolshevik propaganda often used the racially-inflected stereotype of the "Russian barbarian." This cartoon was not just a comment on events in Russia, but had special relevance for America's domestic politics in the period called "The Red Scare" of 1919–20, a phase of factory strikes and civil disobedience throughout the United States. In the conservative press these were often blamed on the influence of the Russian revolution and on the influx of immigrants, especially Russians, Mexicans, and Jews from Eastern Europe.

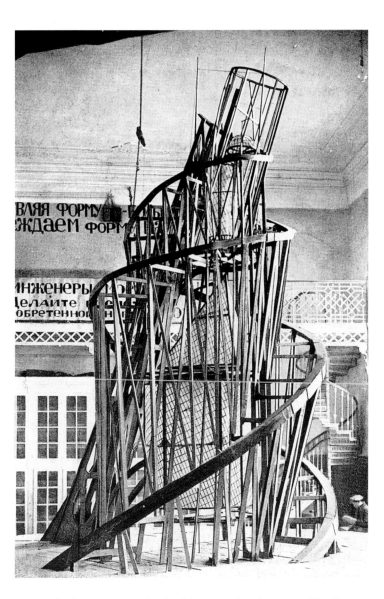

50. Vladimir Tatlin
Model of the Monument to the Third International, on exhibition in Moscow, 1920.

Tatlin's tower reveals a highly centralized vision of both government and propaganda and it typified the Russian avant-garde's naïve enthusiasm for mass-media technology. Tatlin's friend, the poet Velimir Khlebnikov (1885-1922), called the radio "the main tree of consciousness;" "The radio will forge the broken links of the world soul and fuse together all mankind." In cinema, photography, and graphic design, techniques of montage were developed to high levels of sophistication in the 1920s by avant-garde film-makers such as Sergei Eisenstein (1898-1948) and designers such as Gustav Klucis (1895-c. 1944), Aleksandr Rodchenko (1891-1956), Varvara Stepanova (1894-1958) and the Stenberg brothers

(Georgy, 1900-33, and Vladimir, 1899-1982) (FIGS 51, 52, and 53). The avant-garde artists of the Russian Constructivist movement, of which Tatlin was a founding figure, viewed design practices linked to mass production as a means of integrating art with the reconstruction of society. With designs for communist clothing, textiles, furniture, architecture, and even entire cities, Constructivists sought the creation of a total design aesthetic for changing the behavioural habits of the Soviet population, or, as they called it, for "organizing the psyche of the masses." Because of the low levels of industrial technology and materials, few Constructivist designs went into production. By the late 1920s, the Constructivists' vision for their project veered between a radical utopianism and a sinister fantasy of social engineering. On the one hand, Tatlin's design for an "air-bicycle," a human-powered flying machine based on bird anatomy, was devised for the physical and perceptual liberation of the travelling worker – unfortunately his prototype failed to fly. On the other, there were plans

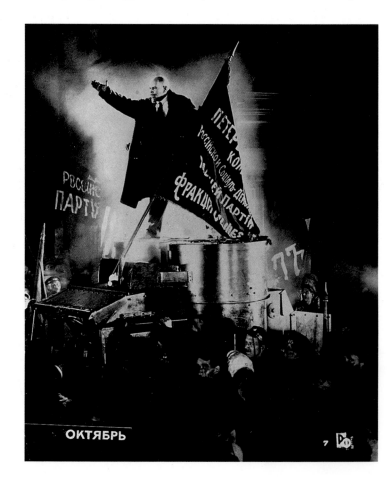

51. *October*, directed by Sergei Eisenstein, 1927, released 1928. Film still.

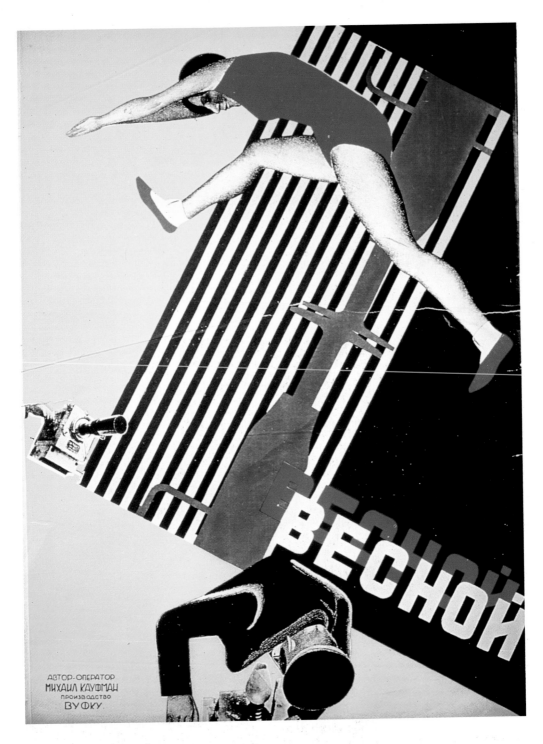

52. Vladimir and Georgy Stenberg
Poster for the film *Springtime* (*Vesnoi*), 1930.

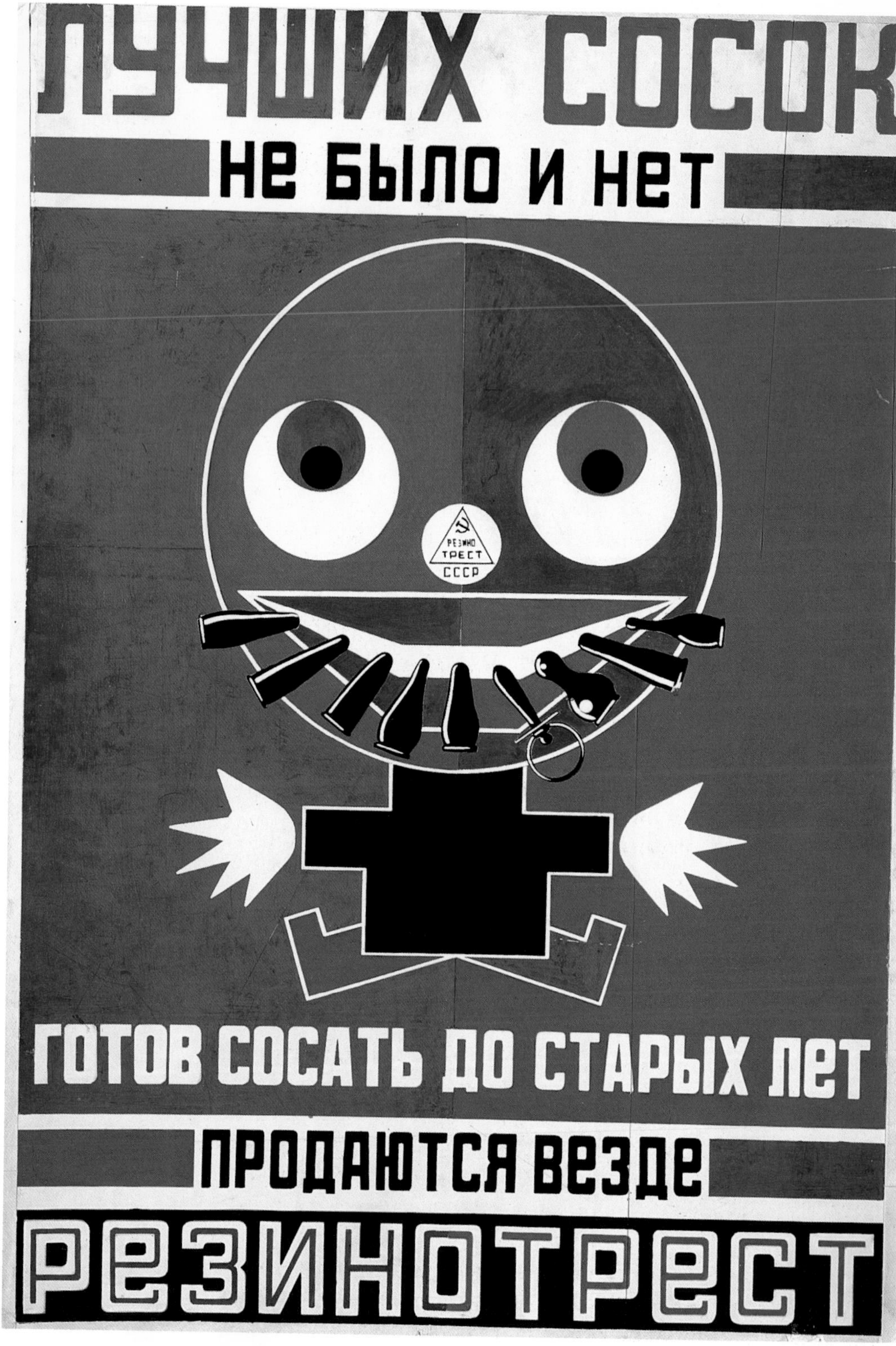
ЛУЧШИХ СОСОК
НЕ БЫЛО И НЕТ
РЕЗИНО ТРЕСТ СССР
ГОТОВ СОСАТЬ ДО СТАРЫХ ЛЕТ
ПРОДАЮТСЯ ВЕЗДЕ
РЕЗИНОТРЕСТ

in Constructivist architecture to enforce communal living in vast housing blocks where private habits could be rigorously policed, children would be raised collectively, and, in one proposal, residents would carry out all activities (including sex) according to a twenty-four-hour timetable.

Between Lenin's death in 1924 and Stalin's rise to power some five years later, the Party leadership maintained its policy of permitting relative pluralism in the arts, but it became increasingly clear that realist approaches were officially favoured more than the avant-garde's experiments. Among the many artistic groups of the 1920s, the Association of Artists of Revolutionary Russia (AKhRR) had been the largest, and gained support for its realist art among influential trade union and Red Army officials. In 1928 the party launched the Cultural Revolution, which aimed to reinvigorate the revolutionary process, and was expressed by a drive to "proletarianize" the arts. Serafima Ryangina's *Red Army Art Studio* (see FIG. 44) captures the mood of the artistic and literary groups which sought to train up a new generation of working-class artists. Some of the leaders of these groups, themselves often middle-class and too young to have been involved in the original revolution and civil war, took to shaving their heads and wearing khaki fatigues to express their militant "class-war" spirit. This prepared the ground for the autocratic cultural policies of Stalinism.

The Theory and Practice of Socialist Realism

The definition and enshrinement of Socialist Realism as the only officially sanctioned approach in art was announced at the first All Union Congress of Soviet Writers in 1934, and had been preceded by the abolition of independent art groups in 1932. It accompanied the new imposition of communist orthodoxies in all fields, including science, medicine, and education. The doctrines were justified theoretically by dubious reinterpretations of both Marxist theory and Russian cultural history. Thus it was claimed that Socialist Realism was a natural continuation of Russia's radical heritage. Nineteenth-century revolutionaries like Nikolai Chernyshevsky (1828-89), author of *The Aesthetic Relations of Art and Reality* (1853) and of Lenin's favourite novel *What is to be Done?* (1863), had upheld realism in art as a moral principle: The artist's duty is to interpret, reflect and change reality. *Bargehaulers on the Volga* (FIG. 54) by Ilya Repin (1844-1930) typified this ethos, and was one of the most famous paintings by the group of socially committed artists opposed to Tsarism known as the *Peredvizhniki*, the "Wanderers" or "Itinerants," because from

53. ALEKSANDR RODCHENKO Advertisement for Rubber Trust babies' dummies, 1923. The text written by the poet Vladimir Mayakovsky, reads: "There have never been and are no better dummies. You will want to suck them until old age."

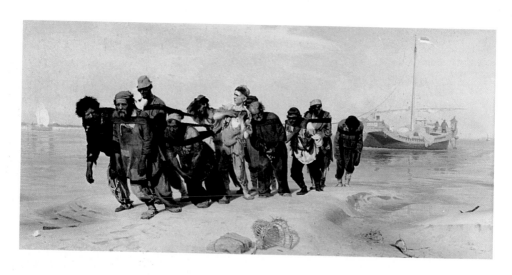

54. ILYA REPIN
Bargehaulers on the Volga,
1870–73. Oil on canvas,
4'3" x 9'2" (1.32 x 2.81 m).
State Russian Museum, St
Petersburg.

Repin spent the summer of
1870 on the banks of the
Volga getting acquainted
with and sketching the
boatmen. It was common
for radical critics in the
nineteenth century to
extrapolate political
messages from details found
in paintings like this. One
critic pointed to the fair-
haired boy who stands out
in his youth and defiant
attitude; he was said to
exemplify the surviving
spark of the people's hope
and resistance.

the mid-1860s they took their art to the provinces in travelling
exhibitions. Repin's picture shows the use of peasants as human
beasts of burden. He said that he aimed "to criticize mercilessly all
the monstrosities of our vile society."

Corn (FIG. 55) by Tatyana Yablonskaya (b. 1917) is a typical
example of Socialist Realism, and its stylistic resemblance to Repin's
work is no accident. Yablonskaya produced the painting shortly
after being rebuked in a magazine for having succumbed in her
earlier work to Impressionism, then held officially to be a deviant
type of foreign influence. On exhibiting *Corn* in 1950 she published a statement accepting this criticism and described how on
a recent visit to a collective farm – in effect, a symbolic renewal
of contact with the "reality" of land and people – she realized that
a picture should start from content, not formal concerns. Reha-
bilitated by this apology, she was awarded a Stalin prize at the
exhibition. Like Repin, she depicts a scene of work, but there is
no hint of hardship; rather, work under the Soviet system is shown
to be joyful and inspiring. There is an air of warm communal-
ity among the women workers, whose faces glow with pride
and socialist fervour. The colour red, dispersed through the painting, harmonizes the composition while symbolizing the political unity of the people (though with the prudishness characteristic of Socialist Realism, the women are spatially segregated from
the men in the background).

It is not entirely impossible that Yablonskaya encountered a
scene like this on her visit to the collective farm, though at the
time this superabundance of food and hi-tech farming equipment
might have been more readily found in art than in real life. Yet
her picture is not meant to show ordinary reality but *socialist*

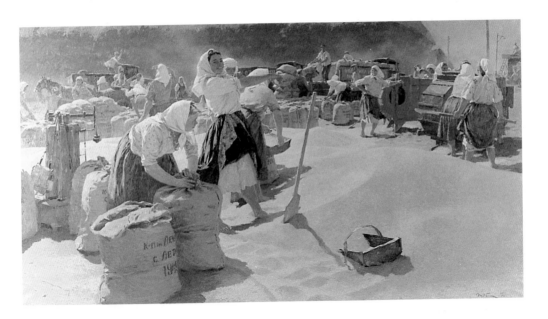

reality: the view of the world interpreted through socialism as defined by the Communist Party. In contrast with Repin's critical realism of the Tsarist period, Yablonskaya's aim is to show, through images of the best aspects of the present, the underlying forces of progress which lead to the future. The theory of Socialist Realism insists that the power to identify and control the direction of this historic progression, and therefore to determine the correct representation of reality, is the exclusive property of the Communist Party. To its theorists, the idea that Socialist Realism is old-fashioned in style is irrelevant, for it is founded on four universal principles: *narodnost* (literally people-ness; accessible to popular audiences and reflecting their concerns); *klassovost* (class-ness; expressing class interests); *ideinost* (using topics relating to concrete current issues); and *partiinost* (party-ness; faithful to the Party's point of view). These principles were drawn from traditions of Russian Populist, Marxist and Leninist ideas, though the legislative authority which they acquired was strictly Stalinist.

55. Tatyana Yablonskaya
Corn, 1949. Oil on canvas,
6'7" x 12'1" (2 x 3.7 m).
Tretyakov Gallery,
Moscow.

Emblems of Soviet Heroism

In paintings, novels, and films, Socialist Realism created a parallel world peopled by heroes and heroines who personified political ideals. As tireless labourers, courageous Red Army soldiers, diligent schoolchildren or dedicated Party activists, they demonstrated exemplary behaviour and the attitudes of perfect citizens. The concept of the New Soviet Person was in part descended

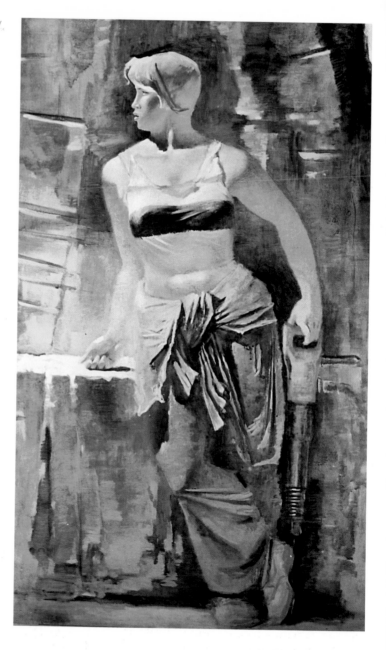

56. ALEKSANDR SAMOKHVALOV
*Woman Metro-Builder with
a Pneumatic Drill*, 1937.
Oil on canvas, 6'8" x 4'3"
(2.05 x 1.3 m). State Russian
Museum, St Petersburg.

from the original Marxist belief that a harmonious society in the future would enable the full development of the individual. This predicted the mental, moral, and physical improvement of humanity as a long-term and collective endeavour. Under Stalinism the idea became authoritarian and didactic, promoting an élitist cult of superhuman individuals whose powers matched the epic tasks of socialist construction. *Woman Metro-Builder with a Pneumatic Drill* (FIG. 56) by Aleksandr Samokhvalov (1894-1971) represents the new athlete of labour, whose real-life versions, the Stakhanovites, were becoming media celebrities. The Stakhanovites were a new class of specially selected and highly-paid work champions named after the coal-miner Aleksei Stakhanov, who in 1935 had allegedly dug up 102 tons of coal in a single night-shift. They were compared with Prometheus and the *bogatyr*, the hero of Russian folklore. This rhetoric matched the atmosphere of the Second Five Year Plan, 1932-36, which set wild production quotas for factories and farms and imposed severe punishments on those who failed to reach them. As part of the Plan, and a feature of the grandiose rebuilding of Moscow, the new Metro system which opened in 1935 was a prestigious symbol of Stalinist achievement. Samokhvalov's Metro-builder embodies this achievement like a female Hercules in the underworld. Though the painting attests to the involvement of women in the workplace, Stalinism had replaced the residue of early Bolshevik feminism with conservative family values. Despite the large proportion of women among industrial workers, most Stakhanovites were men and their wives were urged to become "housewife-activists."

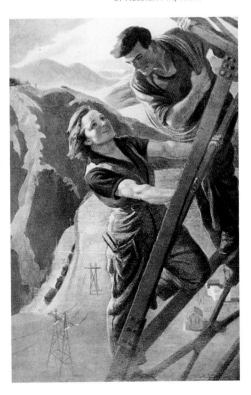

57. SERAFIMA RYANGINA
Higher and Higher, 1934.
Oil on canvas, 4'10" x 3'3"
(1.49 x 1 m). State Museum
of Russian Art, Kiev.

Higher and Higher (FIG. 57) by Serafima Ryangina (1891-1955), showing two young electrical workers climbing a pylon high above the countryside, also valorizes one of the earliest Soviet development projects, the building of an electricity network across the nation. Started by Lenin, the State Electrification Campaign was imbued with symbolic significance. It evoked the spread of light, power and energy across the nation, the mastering of the wilderness, and the unification of remote rural communities with the industrial and political centres of power. The painting's style adapts the imagery of mass culture, combining the Hollywood looks of the couple with a composition that resembles a capitalist advertisement or the illustration of a popular novel of romance and adventure. But the relationship between the man and woman, poised like mountaineers, is beyond erotic attachment. The euphoric gaze of the woman is directed upwards to a point in the distance. This formulaic forwards-and-upwards look, which recurs in the codes of Socialist Realism, signifies a

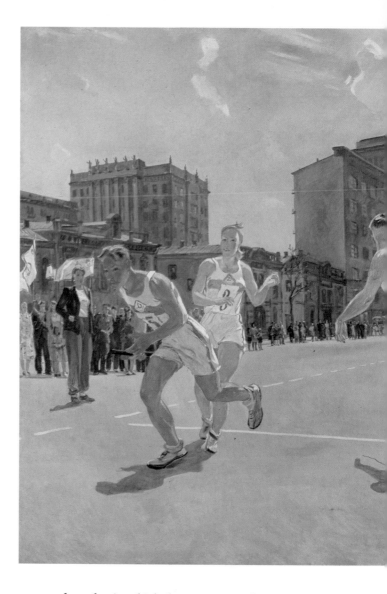

temporal overlap in which the present is infused with the spirit of the future. Representations in art and the media of the labourers who worked on construction projects in remote districts often portrayed them as a breed of pioneers on a new frontier. Even landscape paintings, which at first sight would seem free of ideological meanings, often included electricity pylons or a train as signs of the triumph of progress over nature. In reality, though, the vast industrial projects of the 1930s involved the conscription, for "re-education," of hundreds of thousands of convict labourers, including political dissidents. Many of them died under the harsh working conditions.

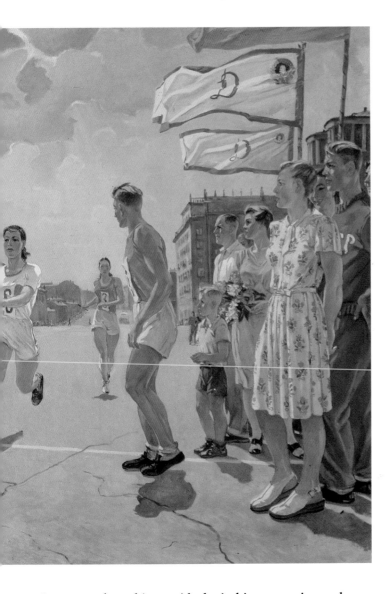

58. ALEKSANDR DEINEKA
*A Relay Race Around the
"B" Ring*, 1947. Oil on
canvas, 6'6" x 9'9" (1.98 x
2.97 m). Tretyakov Gallery,
Moscow.

Sport was also subject to ideological interpretation and control. Sport signified wholesome and improving endeavour, which, like work, directs collective energy into achievement-seeking pursuits. *A Relay Race Around the "B" Ring* (FIG. 58) by Aleksandr Deineka (1899-1969) records the type of sporting occasion that was a constant and often compulsory feature of life. Such events were partly intended to limit opportunities for solitary leisure, which was frowned upon, and to cultivate enthusiasm for physical exertion. The functions of sport in Soviet society were similar to those in Nazi Germany, but the Soviet sport ethos placed less emphasis on the perfection and beauty of the individual

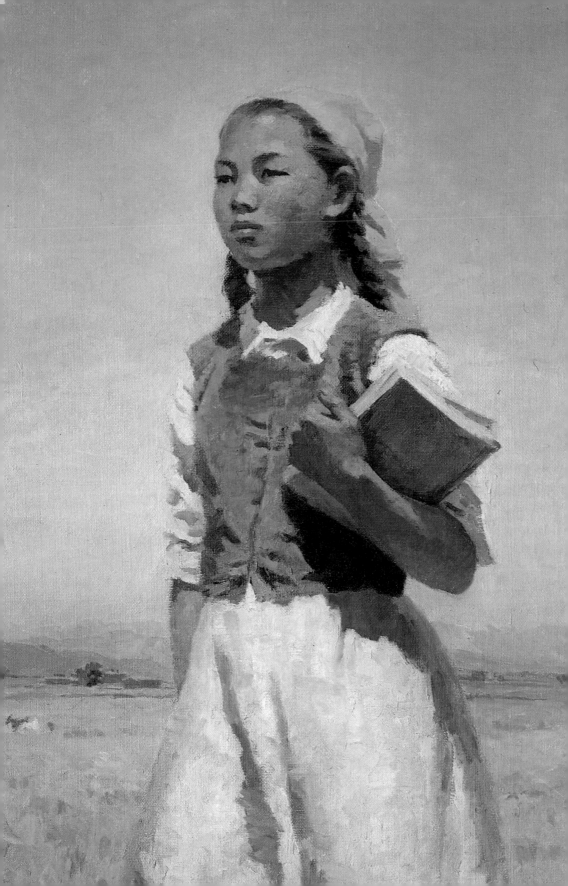

athlete's body, which in the Third Reich, as noted earlier, was a vehicle for Nazi concepts of racial supremacy. In Russia's early Bolshevik period, there had been a movement within the Party to abolish competitive sports altogether and to foster only communal forms of exercise. This was suppressed under Stalin, but the nationwide campaigns to improve the health, hygiene, and fitness of adults and children continued. Throughout the Soviet period, the view of sport was inseparable from that of work, and therefore directly linked to the state's economic aims. Like the material instruments of its factories and farms, the bodies of Soviet people were regarded as elements of the nation's "productive forces."

Although Soviet propaganda was effectively directed by Moscow, its audiences reached far beyond Russia to the Soviet republics of eastern Europe and across Asia, embracing many ethnic groups with different languages and religions. Their control by Soviet power was a continuation of Tsarist imperialism. Stalinist cultural policy vacillated in its view of the non-Russian republics. While the principle of *narodnost* (people-ness) implied some respect for local folk traditions, this was usually waived by Moscow's impulse to spread Russian-oriented conformity. The work of Semen Chuykov (1902-80), who was born in the Asian republic of Kirgizia and educated in Moscow, typified a mild adaptation of Socialist Realism to non-Russian themes. His painting *A Daughter of Soviet Kirgizia* (FIG. 59), awarded a Stalin prize in 1949, is another emblem of ideal citizenship composed of an amalgamation of standard ideological signs. The schoolgirl's steadfast gaze and forward-march indicate, alongside her exemplary eagerness to go to school, the quality of progress which her education represents. The way she carries her books in the crook of her elbow is an equally conventional gesture, derived ultimately from traditional images of biblical prophets, and often found in depictions of Marx and Lenin. Like them, she is "the bearer of the doctrine," and she wears as the outward mark of her political enlightenment a red scarf and Western-style clothes. The figure's function as an icon of young communism is combined with its role as the personification of Kirgizia. For this, youthfulness and femininity serve to fix the small, weak, "developing" daughter-republic in a subordinate relationship to Russian power.

Carpet-Weavers of Armenia Weaving a Carpet with a Portrait of Comrade Stalin (FIG. 60) by Mariam Aslamazyan (b. 1907) is also complicit with the cynical double-standards of Moscow's cultural colonization of the non-Russian republics. The loose, decorative style would normally have been censured for its lack of realism but was permitted here as a concession to the "exotic" subject-matter.

Opposite
59. SEMEN CHUYKOV
A Daughter of Soviet Kirgizia, 1948. Oil on canvas, 47" x 13½" (120 x 95 cm). Tretyakov Gallery, Moscow.

Children both symbolized the new society and were the targets of propaganda. An early Communist Party directive had stipulated: "Children's literature must be militantly Bolshevik, a call to struggle and to victory. The children's books must portray the Socialist transformation of the country and the people in bright and imaginative forms, bringing up the children in the spirit of proletarian internationalism."

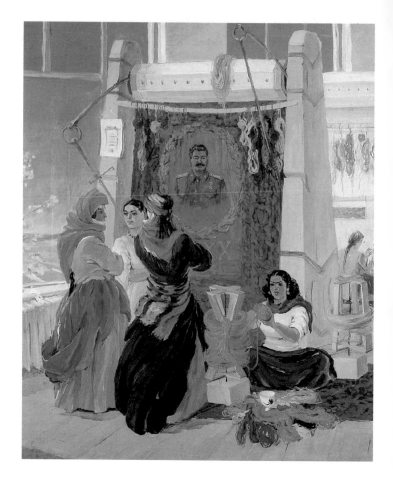

60. MARIAM ASLAMAZYAN
*Carpet-Weavers of Armenia
Weaving a Carpet with a
Portrait of Comrade Stalin*,
1950. Oil on canvas, 4'11"
x 4'1" (1.5 x 1.24 m).
Armenian Gallery of Fine
Arts, Erevan.

The painting shows a craft workshop in Armenia making the type of state-commissioned ornament used to decorate public buildings and government offices. It seems to allude to folk traditions only to demonstrate their actual annihilation by Stalinist kitsch.

The greatest hero in Stalinist culture was, of course, Stalin himself. The personality cult invented to revere the supreme achievements and qualities of Stalin matched in scale and extravagance those devoted to Hitler and Mussolini, although a cult of leadership had no basis in Marxist thought. Lenin was opposed to the creation of his own personality cult, and seems to have had a genuine distaste for the élitism and individualism which it would imply. The elevation of Lenin to saintly or godlike status greatly accelerated after his death and was largely instigated by Stalin as a means to justify his own stature as Lenin's successor. Stalinism was able to harness the old legacy of Tsar-worship which had been nurtured since the Middle Ages in Russian peasant folklore. Many images portrayed Stalin as a benevolent patriarch, often showing him in the company of workers, soldiers, or politicians upon whom he bestows his fatherly attention and words of wisdom. In *Stalin's Speech at the 16th Congress of the Communist Party* (FIG. 61), Aleksandr Gerasimov (1881-1963) depicted Stalin in a church-like atmosphere in front of the sacred effigy of Lenin.

Stalin employed a stable of court painters to produce hundreds of official portraits, some of which were of immense size and painted by brigades of artists working under production-line conditions. The financial rewards and privileges for favoured artists could be substantial, but painting Stalin was a dangerous occupation. Those who worked closely with him, such as his political colleagues, secretaries, interpreters, and bodyguards, had a tendency to "disappear," to be arrested, executed, or secretly murdered according to his paranoid whims. In reality, Stalin was short, fat, and bandy-legged with a pock-marked face, narrow forehead, and withered left arm. But an official artist would have been unwise to depict his physical appearance with any degree of accuracy.

As a young man at the time of the October Revolution, Stalin had played no more than a peripheral part in the Bolshevik uprising. This potentially embarrassing fact was glossed over by fictional biographies, which exaggerated the revolutionary adventures of his youth, and described his warm friendship with Lenin. Evidence in fact suggests that Lenin viewed him with distrust and personal dislike. Stalin, in turn, came to fear all the "Old Bolsheviks" and anyone who had been involved in the original

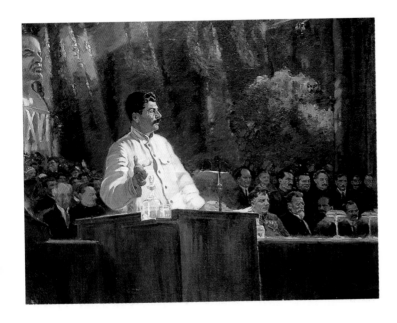

61. ALEKSANDR GERASIMOV
Sketch for *Stalin's Speech at the 16th Congress of the Communist Party*, 1933.
Oil on canvas, 39" x 50" (99.5 x 128 cm). Tretyakov Gallery, Moscow.

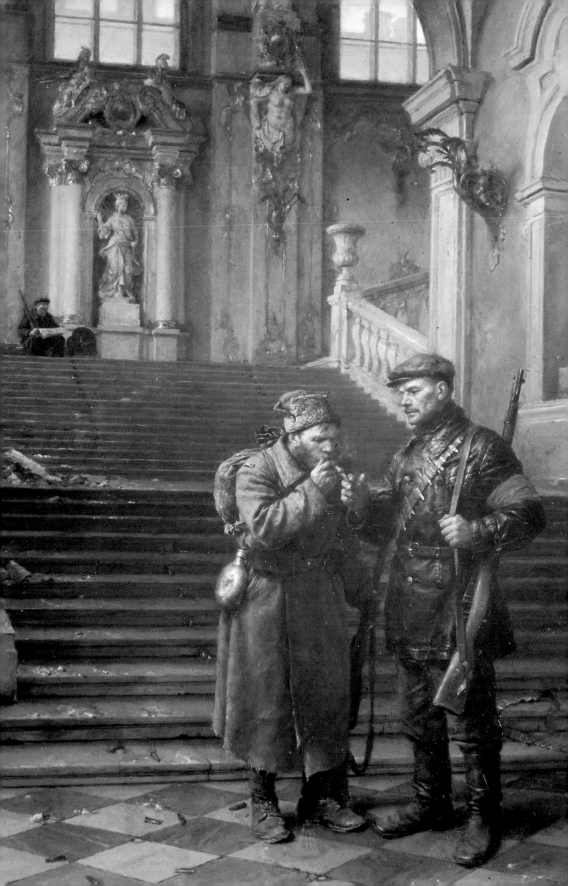

revolutionary movement. From the mid-1930s, he set about purging the Party leadership and armed forces in waves of show trials and mass-executions. Among those caught up was the Constructivist artist Gustav Klucis, who died in a prison camp in 1944, where he was interned for having fought for the Bolsheviks in the Ninth Regiment of Latvian Rifles in 1917. For Socialist Realist history painters, the depiction of the October uprising had to be approached with caution. The historical insurrection had to be recounted in a manner which stressed that the rebellion had been contained, like the continuing revolutionary process under Stalin, by strict obedience, self-discipline, and respect for authority. This conservative revision is seen in *The Winter Palace is Taken* (FIG. 62) by Vladimir Serov (1910-68), which was completed a year after Stalin's death. Two battle-weary soldiers stand in the hall of the captured palace. Spent cartridges at their feet suggest the fading echoes of gunfire. Their victory, rewarded with a quiet cigarette break, marks the pivotal event of Russian history. But it is a sombre scene with an air of order and harmony enhanced by the symmetrical composition and the laborious academic style. Ostensibly, the painting's purpose is to venerate the Workers' State by dignifying its moment of origin, though its effect is to reconstruct that moment as one of grim stasis, drained of rebellious energy.

After Stalin's death in 1953 there was some relaxation of cultural regulations. In February 1956 the new leader, Nikita Khrushchev, formally denounced Stalin at a closed session of the Party Congress, and subsequently thousands of works of art of the Stalinist period, especially those which depicted him, were destroyed or hidden and disappeared from the art history books. Although the excesses of Stalin's personality cult were not repeated by his successors, the heroization of Soviet workers continued as the principal theme of Socialist Realism. *Builders of the Bratsk Hydroelectric Power Station* (FIG. 63) by Viktor Popkov lines up the stock characters and assigns to them their required qualities; even while taking a work-break they look sober, industrious, and vigilant. But during the 1960s and 1970s nonconformist and dissident art groups were increasingly active. Technically, it had never been illegal for an artist to work in unorthodox styles, but attempts to exhibit outside the official framework frequently met with police harassment. In the 1970s numerous small exhibitions were held in defiance of Party regulations and were duly closed down, sometimes within hours of opening. In Moscow in September 1974, an open-air exhibition on a patch of suburban wasteland was broken up by bulldozers and water cannons. The "Bulldozer Exhibition" was widely reported in the Western press.

Opposite
62. VLADIMIR SEROV
The Winter Palace is Taken,
1954. Oil on canvas, 33 x
27¾" (84 x 70.4 cm).
Tretyakov Gallery, Moscow.

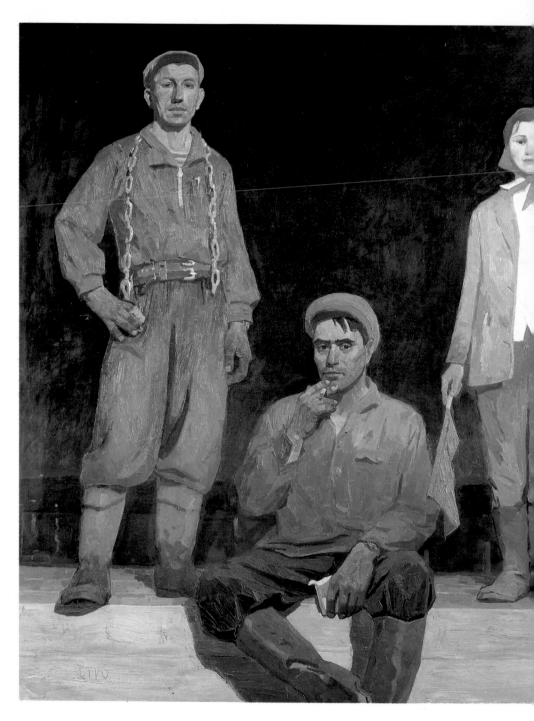

63. Viktor Popkov
Builders of the Bratsk Hydroelectric Power Station,
1961. Oil on canvas, 6' x 9'10" (1.83 x 3 m).
Tretyakov Gallery, Moscow.

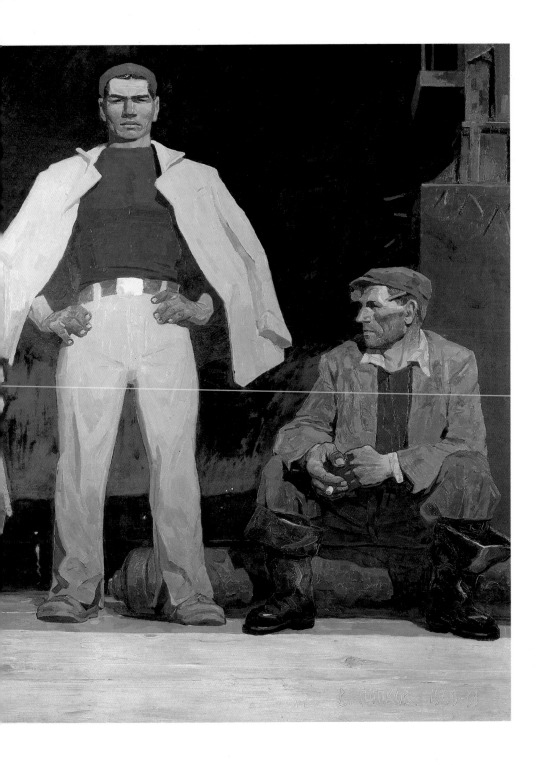

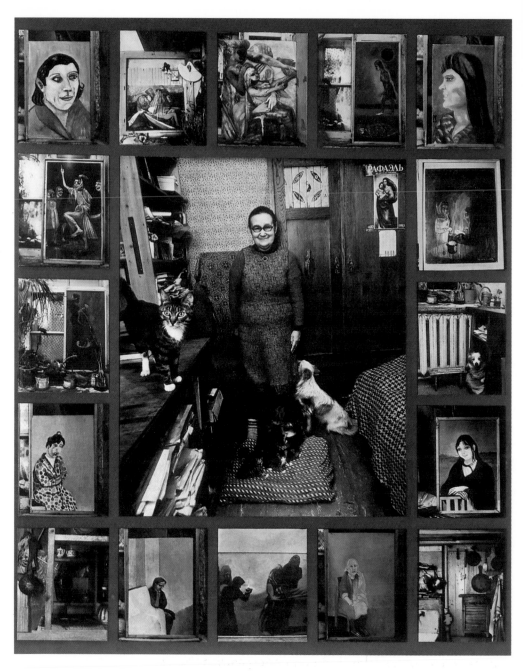

64. NATALIA TSEKHOMSKAYA
The Artist Lenina Nikitina, 1984. Gelatin silver
print with watercolour and ink additions, 44 x
30" (59.4 x 49.1 cm). The Norton and Nancy
Dodge Collection, The Jane Voorhees
Zimmerli Art Museum, Rutgers, The State
University of New Jersey.

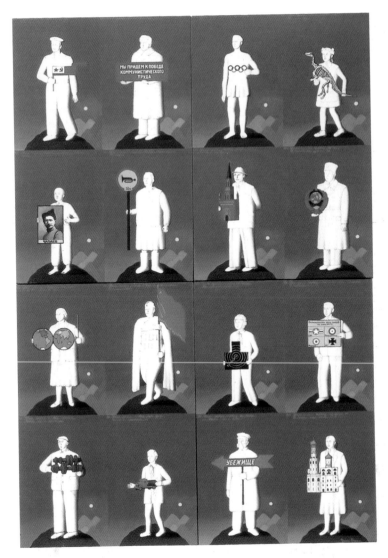

65. GRISHA BRUSKIN
Fragment from Part III of the
"Fundamental Lexicon",
1986. Oil on linen, 23 x
19" (112 x 76.5 cm). The
Norton and Nancy Dodge
Collection, The Jane
Voorhees Zimmerli Art
Museum, Rutgers, The State
University of New Jersey.

Nonconformist art has covered a wide variety of styles and themes.
Lenina Nikitina (b. 1931), for example, has devoted much of
her work to exploring her memories of the 900-day siege of
Leningrad in the Second World War, during which she was
witness to the death by starvation of her mother and sister. Her
survival and work are recorded in the composite portrait by Natalia
Tsekhomskaya (FIG. 64). The paintings and sculptures of Grisha
Bruskin (b. 1945) comment critically on Socialist Realist formulae. His serial piece, the *Fundamental Lexicon* (FIG. 65) is a visual
catalogue of the symbols and stereotypes of official Soviet culture.
With its deadpan literalism, it lays bare the ideological sign systems of communist state art.

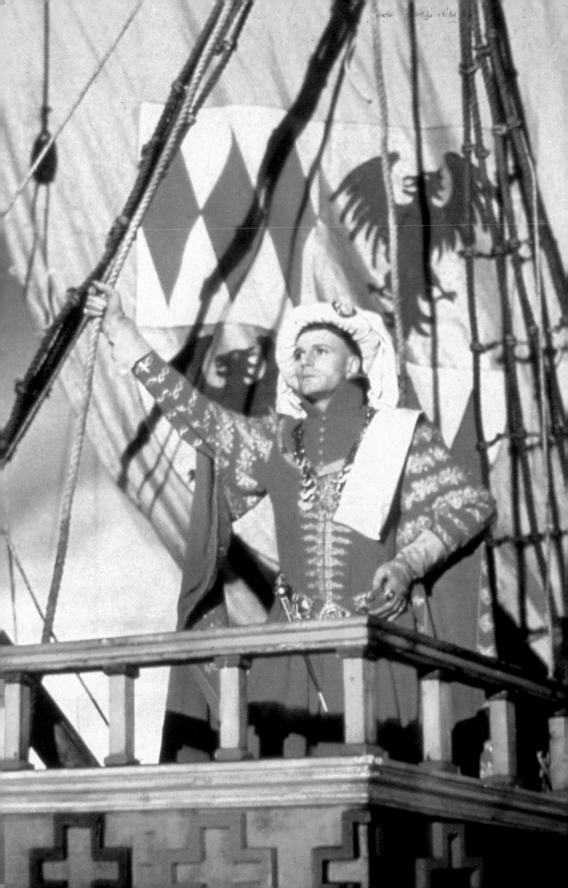

FOUR

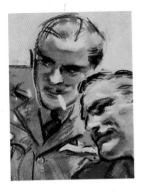

Propaganda at War

artime propaganda attempts to make people adjust to abnormal conditions, and adapt their priorities and moral standards to accommodate the needs of war. To achieve this, propagandists have often represented warfare by using conventional visual codes already established in mass culture. Thus, recruitment posters have often been designed to look like advertisements or movie posters. Propaganda films have used the formulae of westerns and crime dramas. Film stars, singers, sports personalities, and cartoon characters have been enlisted to propagate the official messages of the war effort. The effect of this has been to make war seem familiar and at the same time to glamorize it by exploiting the habits of fantasy and desire generated by mass entertainment. This process is usually accompanied by the rigorous censorship of alternative representations.

The role of traditional forms of art, such as painting, sculpture, and theatre, has been relatively marginal. Where art functions in war propaganda, it is often as a general signifier of a nation's identity, symbolizing its customs and cultural heritage. In some instances, the values of artistic heritage could be preserved within mass culture. For example, the film of Shakespeare's *Henry V*, directed by and starring Laurence Olivier and released in Britain in 1945 (FIG. 66), brought to mass audiences a quintessential historical vision of Englishness, encapsulated by martial triumph, royal pageantry, and the spirit of Shakespeare himself, representing the peak of English culture. Here, a conception of national culture features as the symbolic territory defended in war.

The First World War was the first "total war." In contrast with nineteenth-century wars, which had mainly been fought by small professional armies, the Great War mobilized entire populations for the trenches and for war-effort tasks on the domestic front. Aerial bombing and long-distance shelling further eroded

66. *Henry V*, directed by and starring Laurence Olivier, 1945. Film still.

distinctions between combatants and civilians. Government organizations aimed propaganda at domestic and enemy populations alike, rapidly improvising new techniques which adopted the language and pictorial styles of the popular press, children's fiction, and commercial art. Film, though still in its silent era, was already the leading medium. At the time of the outbreak of war, newsreels were a regular part of cinema programmes. The French industrialist and film producer Charles Pathé (1863-1957) had dominated the world market with his weekly newsreels presented as Pathé-Journal in France and Pathé Gazette in its British and American versions. By 1908, Pathé's company, based in France, was the world's largest film producer, selling twice as many films in the United States as all American film companies put together. The Pathé network began to collapse when the war broke out, but it had already turned the newsreel into an international phenomenon and generated a keen appetite for moving-picture news among cinema audiences across the world.

The nations involved in the war rapidly increased their own production of newsreels, which were heavily inflected with patriotic interpretations of world affairs. Because the newsreel's coming of age coincided with the outbreak of war, the link between movie news and propaganda was firmly established from the outset. German film-making surpassed that of the other combatant nations by retaining some degree of documentary-style realism, but on the whole, wartime newsreels made little pretence of objectivity. Britain's newsreels, made under tight government control, were the most blatantly jingoistic. They often portrayed the war in a global vision of the struggles and triumphs of British imperialism. For example, *The Building of the British Empire* (1917) blended current events with a historical account of the expansion of the Empire, and *What We Are Fighting For* (1918), which focused on the defence of Britain's interests in the Middle East, similarly portrayed the war as a thrilling imperialist adventure. Some films mixed authentic news footage with fictional sequences, such as the American feature *Hearts of the World* (1918), directed by D.W. Griffith (1875-1948). At a time when most film genres leaned towards sensationalist melodrama or slapstick comedy, cinema audiences were not accustomed to expect verisimilitude or respect for the truth.

At the beginning of the Second World War, public responses to propaganda in the Allied countries were more sophisticated. Many of those who remembered the trenches were suspicious of renewed calls to war. However, the methods of manipulating opinion had advanced as well. Techniques developed by the one-party regimes of the Third Reich, fascist Italy and the Soviet Union, where projects of social engineering had become a part of daily life, were readily borrowed by propagandists in the democratic nations. Insistence on the total dedication and sacrifice of individuals to the national cause temporarily introduced to democratic politics a manner of rhetoric that resembled that of the mass-movement ideologies of communism and fascism. Sound cinema and radio proved vital instruments for conveying this message. In addition, propaganda agencies drew on the expertise of advertising, which in turn had advanced between the wars by applying theories from behavioural psychology and the social sciences. The Allied governments developed the practice of carefully monitoring the effects of propaganda, using new market research surveys. These techniques were subsequently adapted by politicians for their election campaigns, and marked a permanent shift towards the image-conscious politics of the television age.

"This Means You": Recruiting Images

Alfred Leete's design for the recruitment poster *Your Country Needs You* (FIG. 67) turned the Secretary for War, Lord Kitchener (1850-1916), into an icon instantly recognizable to the British public. It has almost obliterated any other perception of his career – Margot Asquith, the Prime Minister's wife, once referred to Kitchener as "the great poster." Its format has now become so well known, so often repeated and parodied, that it is hard to reconstruct a sense of its original meanings and effect. But at the time, the poster reflected a real change in views about enlistment and nationalism. British people would have seen patriotic recruitment imagery before, but until 1914 joining the army had been an option only considered by a small minority. For the majority, the affairs of state would have been a remote and separate sphere about which they were neither informed nor consulted. The state had played a relatively small part in regulating everyday life and made few demands on private individuals. In this context, the idea that "your country needs you" would have been a strikingly novel notion for most of its audience. The composition of the

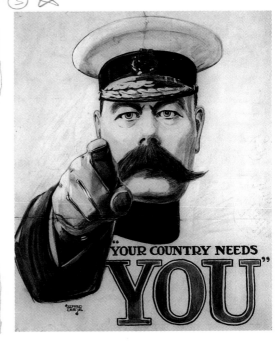

67. ALFRED LEETE
Design for a recruitment poster, *Your Country Needs You*, 1914. Imperial War Museum, London.

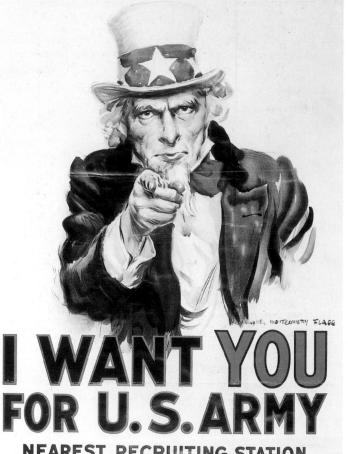

68. JAMES MONTGOMERY
FLAGG
I Want You for U.S. Army,
1917. Poster, 40 x 28″ (101
x 71 cm). Imperial War
Museum, London.

poster, with the remarkably direct address of the disembodied face,
the inescapable eyes, and the pointing finger, highlights this
sudden intensification of the bond between the individual and the
state.

The poster's format was used in many countries, often featuring an allegorical figure rather than a soldier or politician. The
US Army's version of 1917 (FIG. 68) by James Montgomery Flagg
uses Uncle Sam to stand as a composite symbol who personifies
the unity of state and nation as well as the archetypal (white, patriarchal) American. His ferociously authoritarian expression is designed
to leave the viewer in no doubt that American citizenship is a status which carries with it formidable obligations. The moral exhor-
tation takes a similar form in the German poster *Help us Conquer!
Subscribe to the War Loan* (FIG. 69) by Fritz Erler (1868-1940), which

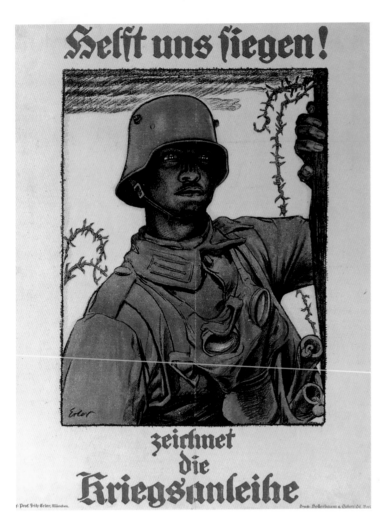

Helft uns siegen!

zeichnet
die
Kriegsanleihe

69. FRITZ ERLER
Help us Conquer!
Subscribe to the War Loan,
(Helft uns siegen! Zeichnet
die Kriegsanleihe) 1917.
Poster, 22¼ x 16½" (56.5 x
41.5 cm). Imperial War
Museum, London.

was released in March 1917 to promote the Sixth War Loan,
and was also produced as a postcard. Erler based the picture on
drawings he had made of soldiers at the front. Again, its most striking feature is the eyes, which gleam as if illuminated from within.
The soldier's steady gaze transcends the bleakest of landscapes
towards his distant goal, one both military and mystical. In the
countries involved in the First World War, there had been a common conception that trench warfare could be in some way an
enlightening and spiritually cleansing experience. Although this
belief gradually dissipated, it had been reinforced by officially
encouraged views that national enlistment would purify and
strengthen the moral fibre of society. Army life would foster both
deference to authority and solidarity between the classes, as
well as counteracting delinquency, alcoholism, and laziness.

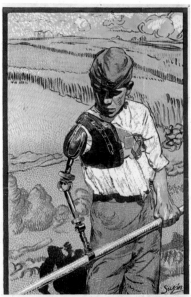

Depictions of the real human cost of war were very rare in this context. The picture of a maimed soldier by the Hungarian artist Pál Suján (b. 1880), made for an exhibition in aid of war relief held in Pozsony in the summer of 1917, has unusual power (FIG. 70). Suján's portrayal of the boy-veteran and the landscape behind him shows an awareness of paintings by Vincent Van Gogh (1853-90), and of other nineteenth-century realist pictures on peasant themes. Though apparently critical of the effects of war, the poster also shows the reintegration of the discharged soldier into the agrarian economy, where he has returned to productive labour. In this respect, the picture contrasts, for example, with the savage anger of cartoons by German Dadaist George Grosz (1893-1959), whose drawings in the period immediately after the war often featured disabled veterans as starving beggars discarded by society.

In many recruitment images the idea of defending the nation was combined with defence of the family. Any conflict of national and personal loyalties might be countered by this linking together of duty to country and family. Posters which featured women with children imploring men to fight reiterated the dominant conception of masculinity as protective and femininity as defenceless. The poster *Women of Britain Say Go* (FIG. 71) contrasts the feminized domestic space with the masculine world of action outdoors. Such images may also seek to exploit the experience of maternal authority over young men (many young recruits would still be living with their parents). Here a notion of the motherland blends national with filial duties, as well as representing the family as an underlying force of stability in troubled times. Women did take part in official and voluntary recruitment campaigns. Bernard Shaw remarked with some disgust on the custom of publicly shaming civilian men with a symbol of cowardice: "Civilized young women handing white feathers to all young men who are not in uniform." "Who's for the trench – Are you, my laddie?" demanded popular writer and propagandist Jessie Pope in her jingoistic poem *The Call*. In revenge, Wilfred Owen (1893-1918), whose anti-war poetry described death and mutilation in battle in terrible detail, dedicated his most famous poem, *Dulce et Decorum Est*, "To Jessie Pope."

Although recruitment propaganda aims to appeal to deeply established values, these are often challenged by the new demands of war. For example, the recruitment of women to war work

70. PÁL SUJÁN
National Exhibition for War Relief (Landes-Kriegsfürsorge-Ausstellung), 1917. Poster, 47¹/₂ x 24¹/₂" (120.7 x 62.2 cm). Imperial War Museum, London.

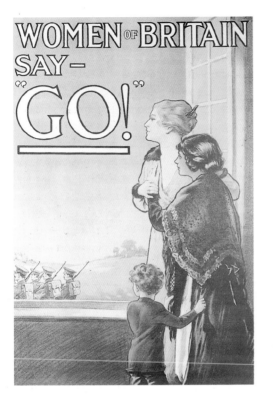

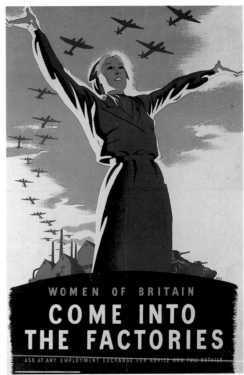

and their involvement in traditional male domains required new roles for women which conflicted with other official images of family and femininity. The British Second World War poster *Women of Britain Come Into the Factories* (FIG. 72) shows an attempt to engage with this problem. The munitions worker gains heroic scale from the low view-point and the upward tilt of her face and eyes. Her outstretched arms welcome the viewer and suggest the V of victory. They also seem to be blessing the tanks and aeroplanes issuing from her factory. Yet the factory itself is relegated to the background and she is removed from it and from the signs of industrial machinery and dirt. The coarseness of her factory outfit is played down; indeed it is made to look attractively modish. The little blue aeroplanes look less like military hardware than a flock of migrating birds, suggesting a link between productivity and the fecundity of nature. The treatment of the factory worker here differs from comparable images of the male worker, which would tend to link him to the machinery of heavy industry and reflect this in his muscularity. Although it shares common features with traditional heroic representations of workers, these have been modified to take account of the gender of its intended audience.

Above left
71. *Women of Britain Say Go*, 1914-19. Poster. Imperial War Museum, London.

Above right
72. *Women of Britain Come Into the Factories*, 1939-45. Poster. Imperial War Museum, London.

The poster seeks to conceal the social conflicts caused by the recruitment of women to industrial war work. Many of the British women who worked in factories and farms, replacing men sent abroad, have recalled the hostility with which they were sometimes treated by male work-mates, some of whom feared that their jobs would be usurped, or that after the war their wages would be reduced to the level of women's pay. In rural communities the presence of single women from the cities was thought improper and a threat to tradition. Much of the propaganda recruiting women to industrial employment tended to stress that this was "for the duration" – an abnormal and temporary expedient. The poster seems to support this by the distant and tenuous link between the woman and the factory, and implies that the worker's femininity has not been diminished. Yet despite encountering antagonism, women war workers have recalled the experience as one which brought them new kinds of freedom and independence. The poster also seems to express this.

73. *Private Joe Louis Says: We're Going to do Our Part – And We'll Win Because We're on God's Side,* 1941-45. Poster. USA, National Archives.

Tensions emerging in recruitment imagery between apparent national unity and actual inequality were evident in matters of race as well as gender. The poster of Joe Louis produced in the United States during the Second World War (FIG. 73) features the world heavyweight boxing champion who had been a national hero since his 1938 defeat of the German champion Max Schmeling. His enlistment soon after the bombing of Pearl Harbor, and his highly publicized involvement in recruitment drives, made him a key figure in the campaign to bring the black community behind the war effort. However, this government campaign relied on vague calls for racial collaboration for the purposes of the war, which contrasted with more committed demands for equality. The American armed forces were strictly segregated, as were most other areas of social life, and recruitment propaganda

which emphasized inter-racial cooperation often faced a hostile reac- Maybe
tion from white audiences and politicians.

Similar contradictions were implicit in the recruitment campaigns mounted by the European nations in their colonies. France,
Germany, Britain, and Belgium all have a long history of recruiting and conscripting African and Asian people to military service:
in effect, an extension of the long-standing practice of forced
labour. It is estimated that approximately 300,000 Africans were
killed in the First World War. The Second World War weakened
Europe's colonial power. This was partly because of the strain
it placed on the resources of colonial administrations. But also,
nationalist propaganda inadvertently increased political awareness
among colonized peoples, and helped to strengthen their own
nationalist demands for independence. Anti-German and anti-
Japanese propaganda used by the French and British colonial authorities attacked their enemies' expansionist aspirations. Ironically,
when addressed to the Asian and African populations who already
lived under European rule, this message only served to intensify
awareness of the politics of anti-racism, and accustomed Asians and
Africans to the possibility of opposing foreign domination through
armed conflict.

Saturation and Censorship

During the Second World War programmes of state propaganda reached an unprecedented scale. After the United States'
entry into the war, the American public was bombarded with war-
related images. For example, the Office of War Information,
founded in June 1942, distributed its major posters in runs of
1.5 million, and posted 100,000 messages in subways, streetcars,
and buses each month. The Army Signal Corps produced 3,000
motion pictures, and distributed 400,000 prints of them. Eventually its films reached 8.5 million viewers every month. In an aver-
age week in American cinemas 50 million viewers watched official
information shorts, and by 1943 nearly one-third of Hollywood
productions were war-theme movies. The US government's information policy combined this prolific production of war imagery
with rigorous censorship that affected all areas of the media.
The newspapers and magazines were supplied with thousands
of photographs from war correspondents and combat photogra-
phers, but before reaching the press these were vetted by a process
of censorship which filtered out photographs of a wide variety
of "unsuitable" topics. It was this process which transformed
the documentary evidence of war into propaganda.

Of taboo images, pictures of dead American servicemen were the most sensitive. Almost all were withheld, though as the war progressed small numbers were strategically released to the press by government agencies with the aim of countering domestic complacency. These were carefully selected – only pictures that conformed with decorous and heroic conventions in the representation of the dead were published. Photographs of wounded American soldiers were rare, too, and were more likely to be published if they showed those who had minor injuries and were being treated, and who looked cheerful (but not too happy about going home). Only references to American casualties caused by enemy action were published. Those caused by accidents, self-inflicted wounds, or "friendly fire" were censored. The depiction of the lifestyle in the services was also censored to exclude brawling, drunkenness, wastefulness, incompetence, and vulgar sexual behaviour. Photographs of soldiers shown suffering acute mental stress were withheld. Pictures of enemy dead were published more readily, but not of civilians killed by American action. Images of enemy peoples in general were controlled to diminish the appearance of shared human qualities – particularly if they were Japanese.

This filtering sought to create an impression that was positive enough to encourage further recruitment, while showing just enough of the soldiers' hardship to maintain commitment in the domestic war effort. Many at the front resented the sanitized imagery that was being conveyed to civilians, and a few of the newspapers themselves criticized censorship policy. But overall the official view that the press should help fight the war rather than report it accurately remained unshaken.

Targeting the Enemy

An Italian poster made in the Second World War (FIG. 74) uses a picture of a black soldier to personify the armed forces of the United States. The soldier, portrayed as a brutish vandal, carries off an antique statue, the *Venus de Milo*, one of the most cherished works of classical art. This crude image was designed to carry a range of connotations for its Italian audience. Partly, it exemplifies the commonplace strategy of representing the enemy as a despoiler of women: Invasion is symbolized in terms of rape. This means of demonizing the enemy has been widely used by nations at war. Numerous posters were produced in both world wars which depict the enemy in the guise of a loutish British Tommy, a Russian barbarian, or a sneering Prussian officer, threatening a woman with rape. In the Italian poster, because the "woman" is a statue, the image more clearly exposes the underlying conceit which presents rape as symbolic of the enemy's assault on national culture (and property). Aiming to manipulate racial prejudice, the choice of a black soldier may have been intended to underscore a propagated view of the inferiority of American culture. In contrast with the purity of Italy's classical heritage, American mass culture – its jazz music, for example – is evoked as one of materialism and decadence.

While images of women often depicted them as innocent victims of enemy aggression, women were also portrayed as the "enemy within," either as unwitting accomplice or deliberate traitor. In

Maybe

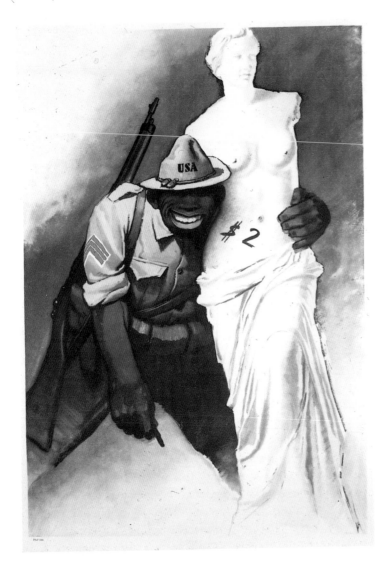

74. GINO BOCCASILE
Italian anti-American poster,
1941-45.

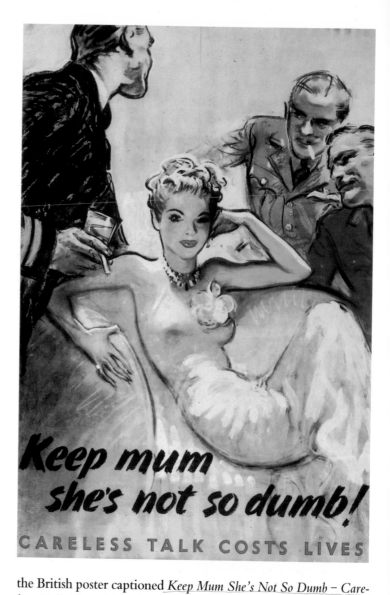

75. *Keep Mum, She's Not So Dumb – Careless Talk Costs Lives*, early 1940s. Poster. Imperial War Museum, London.

the British poster captioned *Keep Mum She's Not So Dumb – Careless Talk Costs Lives* (FIG. 75) an alluring blonde is surrounded by men from the forces in an atmosphere conducive to good conversation. Her knowing look implies that she might repeat any overheard fragments of military information, like troop postings or ship movements, although it does not specify whether she is a spy or just a gossip. Either way, her make-up, jewellery, and silky gown, so out of keeping with the wartime ethos of austerity, signal her moral laxity. All the governments of the combatant nations ran campaigns against careless talk, which implied that the enemy's agents were everywhere. Although these clearly served the real military need to control confidential information, by

① Maybe

embroiling all civilians in a culture of secrecy they also encouraged the public to comply with and foster an official environment of censorship and surveillance.

Enemy populations were also targeted as audiences for propaganda. For this, radio broadcasting was a means of crossing the lines and national borders with misleading or undermining information. American troops fighting the Japanese forces in the Pacific became familiar with the voice of "Tokyo Rose," who was not one woman but a team of twelve who worked as propaganda broadcasters. Mild in technique, their broadcasts from Japanese radio stations were supposed to make the troops feel lonely and homesick by playing American swing music and talking sentimentally about life back in America and the girls they left behind. What effect this had on the GIs' morale would be hard to estimate. The nickname the troops gave to the young Japanese women seems affectionate. But at the end of the war, at least one member of the "Tokyo Rose" team, Iva Toguri D'Aquino, was tried and convicted of treason by the US government. She was imprisoned for six years.

There was also the more crude approach of leaflet drops: "bombing" enemy populations with abusive, subversive, demoralizing, or deceitful printed messages. Often these urged enemy soldiers to surrender and promised them good treatment. All sides active in the Second World War applied the technique. The United States dropped 90 million leaflets in the Far East alone between 1941 and 1945. Most leaflets seem to have been ineffectual – however, the leaflet drop carries one overarching message: Those who can be reached with paper can also be reached with bombs.

War on Television

Although the invention of cinema had brought about a spectacular union of war and mass culture, cinema could not match the immediacy and intimate power of television. Television had become a part of everyday life in most industrialized countries by the early 1950s. But it was the war in Vietnam, from the mid-1960s, which first fully conveyed the explosive mixture of television and warfare to American viewers. News cameras were given unprecedented levels of access to the fields of combat, and at home, to the demonstrations and riots which evidenced the profound social crisis that the war provoked. An awareness of the moral complexities revealed in the television pictures made obsolete the simplistic formulae of Hollywood's traditional war movies. Few Hollywood film companies wanted to tackle the Vietnam War while it was happening. The ardently pro-war *The Green Berets* (FIG. 76) was a relatively rare exception. Produced and co-directed by its star, John Wayne (1907–79), it is essentially a western – the US base which gets raided by the Viet Cong is named "Dodge City." Its format combines the sub-genres of cavalry movie (the Special Forces rescue the outpost) with revenge western (peace-loving lawman is drawn reluctantly into the gunfight). It was released and flopped in 1968, a peak year for anti-war activism among a minority in America, and a time of growing unease among the majority.

There is no doubt that the disquieting pictures sent back from Vietnam played a vital part in raising domestic public concern about the validity and effectiveness of the United States' intervention. But although the television coverage left John Wayne's old-time moralism outmoded, the prevailing tone of the US media's account of the war, especially in its early years, was often one of positive support for the government's war aims. The media's treatment of war footage was quite ambiguous: Although the potentially alarming visual evidence was broadcast with a remarkable lack of restriction, the manner of news presentation was altered

76. *The Green Berets* starring, produced, and co-directed by John Wayne, 1968. Film still.

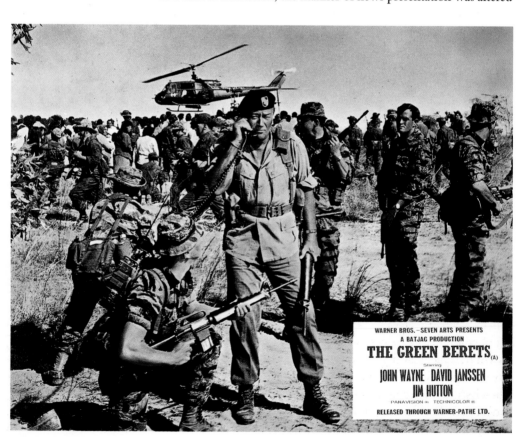

WARNER BROS.–SEVEN ARTS PRESENTS
A BATJAC PRODUCTION
THE GREEN BERETS (A)
Starring
**JOHN WAYNE   DAVID JANSSEN
JIM HUTTON**
PANAVISION ® · TECHNICOLOR ®
RELEASED THROUGH WARNER-PATHE LTD.

to place some limits on its effects. Television pictures of fighting in Vietnam and on riot-torn streets in America were "packaged" by broadcasters in ways designed to lessen their shock effects on audiences. By the late 1960s, a new style of news presentation had become the norm. It was initially known as "Happy Talk." In Happy Talk news, stories are no longer simply read out by a single newsreader, but integrated with an atmosphere of TV studio cheerfulness: friendly banter between presenters; improvised pleasantries about sport and weather; and the tactical use of a closing item on some up-beat heartwarming tale of "human interest." This style reduces any potential sense of critical disruption in social affairs by integrating disturbing pictures and information with a contrived atmosphere of normality.

When the first exchanges of fire broke out in the Gulf War on Wednesday 16 January 1991, President George Bush watched them live on television along with 160 million American viewers. It is said to have been the highest-rating event in American television history. In the following weeks a massive quantity of footage, live reports carried by satellite, and "analysis" by armies of experts poured out of television screens twenty-four hours a day. But this coverage was meticulously managed by a coordinated "information policy" planned between Washington and government leaders of the other Coalition countries. Television reporters were given strict rules: no spontaneous interviews with troops; no pictures of soldiers in "agony or severe shock"; no transmission of "imagery of patients suffering from severe disfigurements." Very few pictures were shown of wounded or killed Iraqi soldiers and civilians. Awareness of these was, in any case, largely neutralized by the new terminology; "surgical bombing" caused merely "collateral damage" (i.e. dead civilians). The precision of the "smart"

77. Desert Storm campaign, Persian Gulf War 1991. Military aerial photograph.

technologies of state-of-the-art weaponry could hardly be questioned in the face of the aerial photographs and video evidence shot by cockpit cameras (FIG. 77). These bloodless pictures, carefully selected and edited, caught the imagination of television viewers (and computer game designers), when the true quantity of explosives dropped in weeks of round-the-clock bombing, and their real effects on their targets, remains unrepresented and unimaginable.

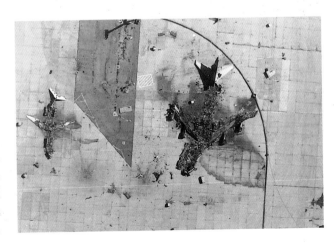

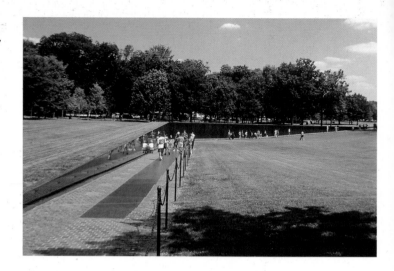

Remembering War: Memorials and Anti-Monuments

How should a war be remembered? Should a war memorial
only commemorate the dead, or should it also be dedicated to the
values they died for? Who has the right to produce commemo-
rative images; is this a task properly left to individuals, or does the
state have an obligation to organize national remembrance and
reconciliation? These questions have opened up tensions between
personal expressions of grief and the public representation of
history. In Britain, for example, during the early stages of the First
World War, small, temporary "street shrines" were created in communities as home-made memorials to the local men killed in
the trenches. Gradually these were replaced by a government programme to coordinate the commissioning of larger memorials.
This aimed to provide more permanent and dignified monuments,
but may also have been motivated by the government's desire
to maintain official control over the imagery of war and nation-
hood and to prevent the street shrines from expressing, as they
sometimes did, critical or oppositional sentiments.

In recent times, no war has provoked as much controversy
in the West as the Vietnam War, and the bitter and painful
divisions in American public opinion were still deep when the first
major memorial was built, the Vietnam Veterans Memorial, designed
by Maya Lin and completed in 1982 (FIGS 78 and 79). The location
chosen for it was the Washington Mall's Constitution Gardens,
a public park near the White House which is laid out with some
of the nation's most famous monuments, including the tall obelisk
of the Washington Monument and the Lincoln Memorial, a

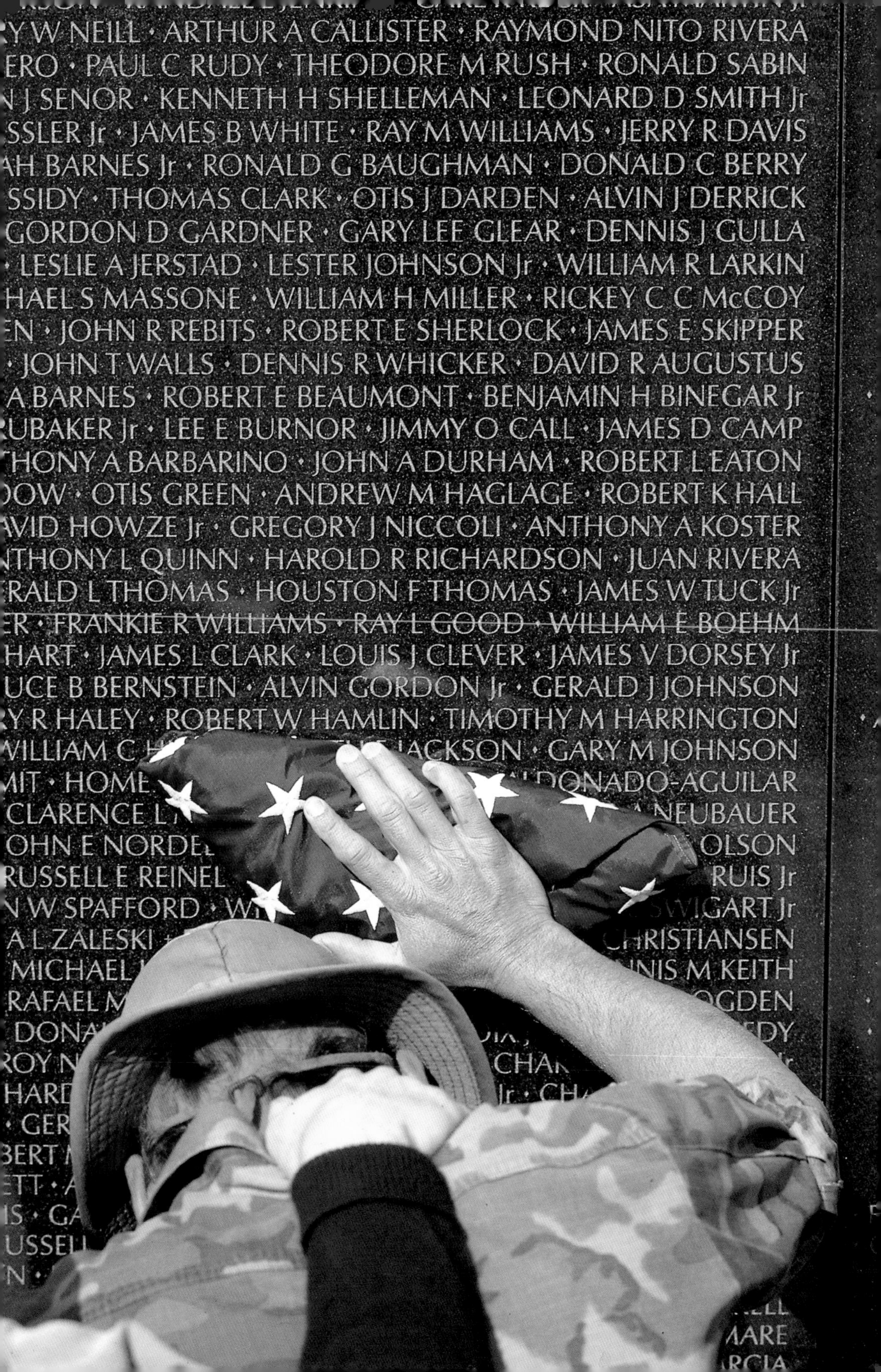
ARTHUR A CALLISTER · RAYMOND NITO RIVERA
PAUL C RUDY · THEODORE M RUSH · RONALD SABIN
KENNETH H SHELLEMAN · LEONARD D SMITH Jr
JAMES B WHITE · RAY M WILLIAMS · JERRY R DAVIS
RONALD G BAUGHMAN · DONALD C BERRY
THOMAS CLARK · OTIS J DARDEN · ALVIN J DERRICK
GORDON D GARDNER · GARY LEE GLEAR · DENNIS J GULLA
LESLIE A JERSTAD · LESTER JOHNSON Jr · WILLIAM R LARKIN
WILLIAM H MILLER · RICKEY C C McCOY
JOHN R REBITS · ROBERT E SHERLOCK · JAMES E SKIPPER
JOHN T WALLS · DENNIS R WHICKER · DAVID R AUGUSTUS
ROBERT E BEAUMONT · BENJAMIN H BINEGAR Jr
LEE E BURNOR · JIMMY O CALL · JAMES D CAMP
JOHN A DURHAM · ROBERT L EATON
OTIS GREEN · ANDREW M HAGLAGE · ROBERT K HALL
GREGORY J NICCOLI · ANTHONY A KOSTER
ANTHONY L QUINN · HAROLD R RICHARDSON · JUAN RIVERA
HOUSTON F THOMAS · JAMES W TUCK Jr
FRANKIE R WILLIAMS · RAY L GOOD · WILLIAM E BOEHM
JAMES L CLARK · LOUIS J CLEVER · JAMES V DORSEY Jr
ALVIN GORDON Jr · GERALD J JOHNSON
ROBERT W HAMLIN · TIMOTHY M HARRINGTON
GARY M JOHNSON
RUSSELL E REINEL

neo-classical temple which houses the seated statue of Abraham Lincoln. The extreme contrast between the grand monuments to America's national heroes and the design of the Vietnam Veterans Memorial provoked strong reactions. One commentator called it a "ditch of shame." The memorial consists of two walls of black granite meeting at an angle of 125 degrees and tapering off at each end. Its back is against the earth, so that viewed from behind, the top of the walls are at ground level, and from a distance it is almost invisible. Its critics opposed it because of its apparent negativity or bleak reticence and its refusal to convey any patriotic or otherwise positive sentiments. But this had been required in the specifications for the original commission, drafted by veterans, which had called for a design which would make no overt political statement, but would simply bear the names of the more than 58,000 American men and women who were killed or went missing in action between 1959 and 1975. Funded through private contributions, the veterans who initiated the project were adamant that it should be dedicated not to the war, nor the nation, but to all those who had served in Vietnam. Specifically, it should *not* be a piece of propaganda. This absence of any positive image or symbol provoked a hostile response from those, like President Reagan's first Secretary for the Interior, James Watt, who insisted that the cause for which the veterans had died should be implicitly praised. As the result of pressure brought to bear, a realistic statue of three American soldiers and a flagpole for the Stars and Stripes were later added nearby.

After winning the competition for the design out of 1,421 anonymous entries, Maya Lin, then a 21-year-old student at Yale University, said that she intended the memorial "to bring out in people the realization of loss and a cathartic healing process." "Brought to a sharper awareness of such loss, it is up to each individual to come to terms with this loss. For death is in the end a personal and private matter and the area contained within this memorial is a quiet place meant for personal reflection and private reckoning." Lin's concept of the memorial as a site for private contemplation underlines the way it declines to be an object of propaganda, because propaganda is usually devised as a form of expression to be received collectively. For a war which so divided public opinion that no image or object could adequately embrace a collective response, the memorial provides instead a text and a space for individual commemoration. It can also serve as a meeting place for small groups, and visitors sometimes attach to it flowers, photographs or messages (some angry and subversive), which are preserved in an archive. The memorial acknowledges, not least by its deliberate contrast with the surrounding monuments, the problematic place which the Vietnam War holds in American history. Its low, intimate, and horizontal format is the formal opposite of the tall, white, and confident structures of the Washington Monument and Lincoln Memorial, though these can be seen reflected in the polished black stone of the walls.

Like an anti-monument, the Vietnam Veterans Memorial creates an alternative to the didactic monologue articulated by traditional built symbols of national identity. A general decline in the tradition of the political public monument reflects a wider dissolution of the idea that "the public" is a unitary category coterminous with "the people" in a national sense. It also reflects the way national histories have been opened to more diverse and contested interpretations. In Germany, artists who have been working on themes of history have engaged in a complex debate about the ethical responsibilities of remembering war and the Holocaust. This has centred on the connotations of the traditional monument, which, in the form of a "thing on a pedestal," has seemed to evince too much of the propaganda style of fascism itself. A monument against fascism might have to be a counter-monument: To oppose the fascist form of public communication, it would need to interact with its public, to accommodate different views, and to counteract myths of unity, destiny, and permanence. Of many recent examples, the *Monument Against Fascism, War and Violence – and for Peace and Human Rights* (FIGS 80 and 81) devised by Jochen Gerz and Esther Shalev-Gerz, and unveiled in Harburg, a suburb of Hamburg in 1986, was a self-critical monument designed to disappear. For the site, the artists declined the park setting originally offered to them, and chose instead an ordinary street location by a shopping centre. The memorial consisted of a pillar 12 metres high and one metre square, made of hollow aluminium plated with a thin layer of soft lead. Like the Vietnam Veterans Memorial, it was unobtrusive from a distance and designed to involve its audience. The artists encouraged passers-by to write their names on the lead surface, testifying to their opposition to fascism and violence. The pillar was designed to be gradually lowered through the ground into a chamber below. While it sank, the upper areas made space for more names, which in turn would slowly disappear. Alongside the names, though, a hubbub of graffiti soon accumulated as people added their own comments, slogans and insignia, colliding anti-fascist with satirical or racist views in a hectic debate carried out in the uncensored language of the streets. The artists had anticipated this vandalism; Gerz said, "Why not give that phenomenon free rein and allow the monument to

80. JOCHEN GERZ and
ESTHER SHALEV-GERZ
*Monument Against Fascism,
War and Violence – and for
Peace and Human Rights,*
Harburg, 1986.

A temporary inscription
near the base said: "We
invite the citizens of
Harburg and visitors to the
town to add their names
here to ours. In doing so,
we commit ourselves to
remain vigilant. As more
and more names cover this
12-metre-tall lead column,
it will gradually be lowered
into the ground. One day it
will have disappeared
completely, and the site of
the Harburg monument
against fascism will be
empty. In the end it is only
ourselves who can rise up
against injustice."

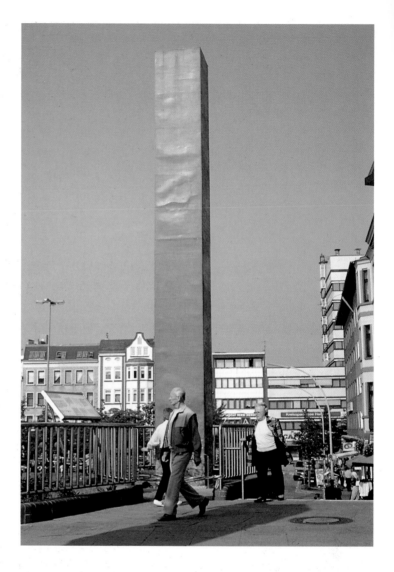

Opposite
81. JOCHEN GERZ and
ESTHER SHALEV-GERZ
*Monument Against Fascism,
War and Violence – and For
Peace and Human Rights*
(detail), Harburg, 1986.

document the social temperament in that way?" And, "What
we did not want was an enormous pedestal with something on
it telling people what they ought to think." In devising the project, the artists had aimed to avoid producing a monument
which sealed up memory, or distanced it from the conflicts of
the present.

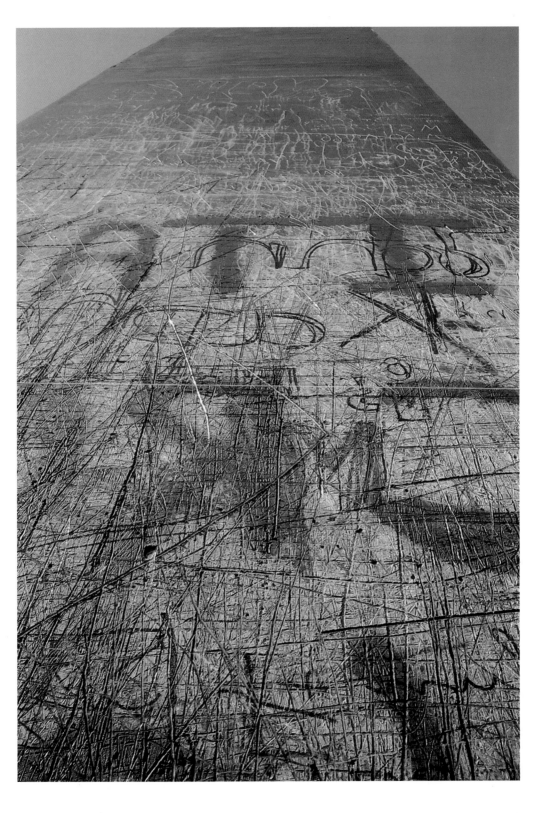

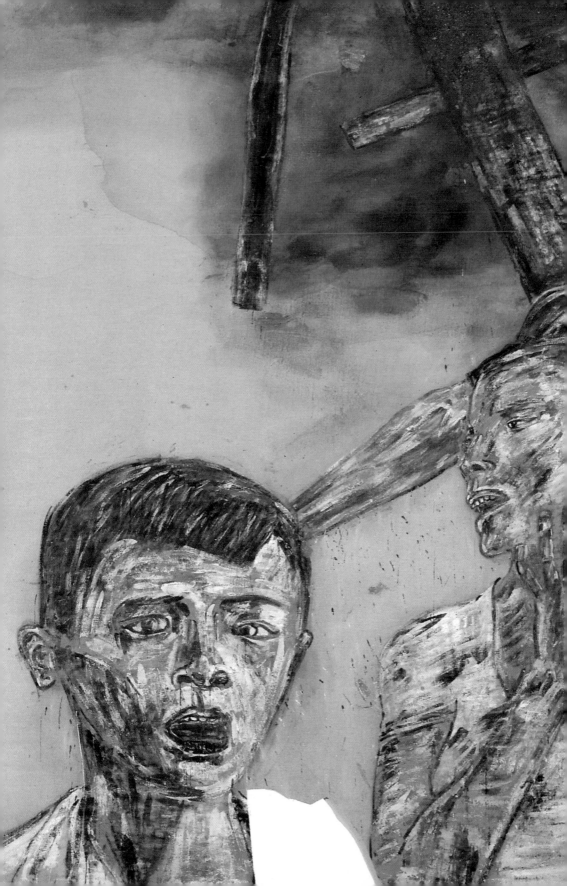

FIVE

The Art of Protest: From Vietnam to AIDS

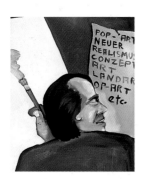

I n May 1967, the artist John Latham was dismissed from his part-time teaching post at St Martin's School of Art in London for destroying the college library's copy of a book of collected essays by Clement Greenberg called *Art and Culture* (1961). At the time, Greenberg was America's most eminent modernist critic, whose writings had helped to promote the aesthetic values of American abstract art, which had gained a very high level of commercial and critical success in the United States and Western Europe. Implicit in Greenberg's position was the view that "true quality" in modern art could only be maintained by the investigation and elaboration of the formal properties of each medium. Thus, painting, his principal concern, should be devoted to exploring relationships between colour, texture, composition, and the flatness of the painted surface. This implied that art should avoid "literariness"; it should not try to send social or political messages. During the 1960s, formalism became dominant in the mainstream of modernist museums and the art market. To its opponents, the doctrine was associated with a cold and dry purist abstraction, exemplified by the "white box" spaces of modernist galleries and museums. Scorning these values, Latham's destruction of Greenberg's book was carried out in the form of an elaborate mock-scientific experiment into the properties of purity and impurity. Helped by his friends, Latham had chewed up the book and spat it out page by page into a glass jar. The chewed pages were then dissolved in sulphuric acid and mixed with sodium

82. LEON GOLUB
Vietnam II, 1973 (detail). Acrylic on canvas, 10 x 40' (3.04 x 1.02 m).

bicarbonate and yeast. After fermenting for nearly a year, the distilled book in its jar was returned to the library, which had sent Latham a postcard with the poignant message: "Wanted urgently by a student, Art and Culture." Latham recovered the jar and exhibited it with the postcard and fermenting equipment under the title *Still and Chew*.

Although Latham's act had made no explicit political statement, it was characteristic of some of the new strategies adopted by artists radicalized during the United States' intervention in the war in Vietnam. Drawing on conceptual and performance art, these would often involve actions which circumvented the usual discourses of art and politics while rejecting the ideal of art's neutrality in the face of political struggles. They were often irreverent and antagonistic, and directed against academic institutions, using the art college or university campus as their forum. For example, in 1970 Terry Fox burned up a large flowerbed in front of Berkeley University's Art Museum with a flamethrower of the type being used in Vietnam. He titled the performance *Defoliation*, in case anyone missed the point. As a "work of art," the action was practically indistinguishable from the everyday incidents of violent protest which revealed the deep crisis in American society. By May 1969 there were official reports of 471 disturbances at 211 colleges during the previous two years; these included 25 bombings, 46 cases of arson, 598 injuries, 6,158 arrests, and 207 buildings occupied. In November 1971 Californian artist Chris Burden got a friend to shoot him in the arm with a rifle. He refused to ascribe a clear intention to the shooting or to later performances: crawling almost naked over broken glass; and having his hands nailed to the roof of a Volkswagen. Part of the meaning of Burden's work lay in the problems of response and responsibility forced on his audience. Should you *watch* someone doing this to themselves? How was it like or unlike watching the newsfootage of killings, burnings, and woundings which had poured out of American televisions since the beginning of the Vietnam War?

"Bringing the War Home" was a current slogan for protesters who perceived militarist imperialism in Southeast Asia as an extension of endemic racism, sexism, and economic exploitation at home. Martha Rosler used the phrase in the title of a series of photomontages in which she juxtaposed violent war images with scenes of middle-class American domesticity. She later recalled, "The 1960s meant the delegitimation of all sorts of institutional fictions, one after another. When I finally understood what it meant to say that the war in Vietnam was not an 'accident,' I virtually stopped painting and started doing agitational works." Rosler refused to be involved in the gallery and market system: "To show anti-war, or feminist agitation in such a setting verged on the obscene, for its site seemed more properly 'the street,' or the underground press where such material could marshal the troops." An early project in an alternative site was the *Peace Tower* designed by sculptor Mark di Suvero and built on a rented lot on the corner of Sunset and La Cienega Boulevards in Los Angeles in 1966 (FIG. 83). Conceived by a group called the Artists Protest Committee, the 60-foot tower was accompanied by 400 small panels sent in by artists from all over the world confirming in words and images their opposition to the war. The following year, the New York collective called Artists and Writers Protest planned Angry Arts Week which, from 29 January to 5 February, saw a festival of art events involving some 600 artists. The organizing group included Leon Golub (b. 1922), whose paintings took on overt

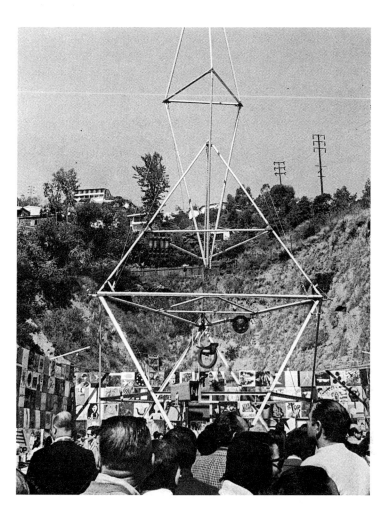

83. MARK DI SUVERO *Peace Tower* in construction, Los Angeles, 1966. Oil and Steel Gallery, Long Island City, New York.

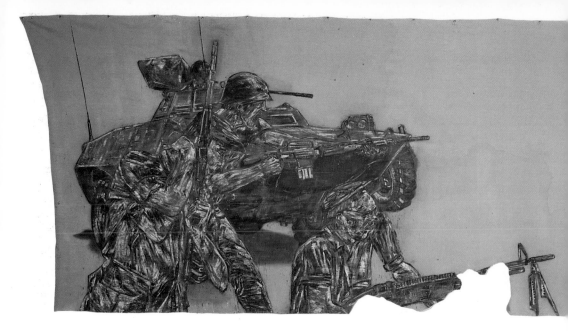

84. LEON GOLUB
Vietnam II, 1973. Acrylic on
canvas, 10′ x 40 ′ (3.04 x
1.02 m).

anti-war themes (FIG. 84), and Nancy Spero (b. 1926), who said,
"the Vietnam war was the primary impetus in rethinking my position as an artist." But despite the level of dissent, relatively few of
the established artists changed the kind of art they had been making since before the war. Outspoken figures in the anti-war movement such as di Suvero, Ad Reinhardt, and Carl Andre continued
to work in abstract and minimalist styles. Arguably, the dominance
of formalist values in American art had left many artists ill-equipped
or disinclined to bring their political views into their artistic practice. However, the events of this period had an important long-
term effect because of the ways they altered perceptions of powerful institutions in the art system.

Of these institutions, New York's Museum of Modern Art,
founded in 1929, became a focus of oppositional scrutiny. One
of the oldest and most prestigious of modernist galleries, MoMA
had championed avant-garde art for decades, often in the face of
right-wing opposition. Its curators had established a "non-politi-
cal" ethic of artistic freedom, persuasively arguing, notably against
McCarthyist censorship in the 1950s, that any attempt to make
art subservient to politics was a type of repression comparable to
that of Nazism or (more pointedly) Stalinism. But by the late 1960s,
a new challenge to this apparent apoliticism targeted MoMA's major
sponsors, the super-rich Rockefeller family, and examined the
museum's function in relation to Rockefeller corporate interests.
In 1969 a group of artists called the Guerrilla Art Action Group produced a leaflet which alleged that the museum was funded by "blood

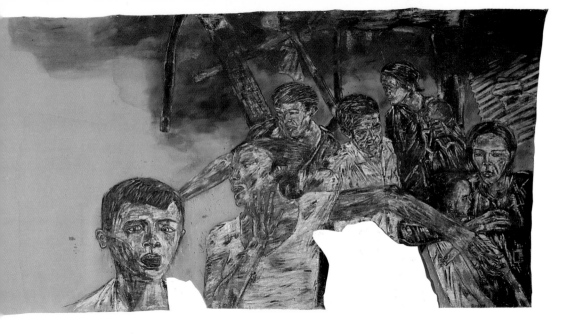

money": "The Standard Oil Corporation of California – which is a special interest of David Rockefeller (Chairman of the Board of Trustees of the Museum of Modern Art) – leased one of its plants to United Technology Center (UTC) for the specific purpose of manufacturing napalm." It also alleged that the Rockefeller brothers owned 20 per cent of the McDonnell Aircraft Corporation, "deeply involved in chemical and biological warfare research." To stress their message, the Guerrilla Art Action Group staged one of their "die in" performances at the museum (FIG. 85).

85. Guerrilla Art Action Group, *A Call for the Immediate Resignation of all the Rockefellers from the Board of the Museum of Modern Art*" ("*Blood Bath*"), New York, November 18, 1969.

Carl Andre, sculptor, Marxist and anti-war activist said in 1970: "The war in Vietnam is not a war for resources, it is a demonstration to the people of the world that they had better not wish to change things radically because if they do, the United States will send an occupying, punishing force … And they wish to run these quiet apolitical institutions like museums and universities suppressing politics among artists, among students, among professors. We are killing people ostensibly to maintain the rationale of artistic freedom."

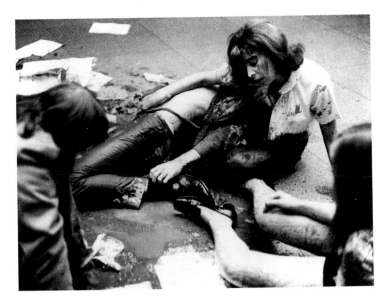

Turning up unannounced, they spread a hundred copies of their leaflet on the floor of the lobby, and then struggled with each other, screaming and shouting "Rape" and tearing at their clothes, bursting open concealed bags of animal blood. They left shortly before the police arrived. Further protests directed at museums culminated in 1970 – a year of bombing in Cambodia and the killing of students in demonstrations at Jackson State College and Kent State University – with an "Art Strike" which called on museums to close down for a day. The Art Workers Coalition (AWC), the main body of anti-war artists, also invited Picasso to remove *Guernica* from MoMA as a protest against the museum's perceived complicity with the Vietnam War. Inevitably, MoMA's director John Hightower told the press that the artists were acting like Hitler and Stalin. A more astute criticism came from Meyer Schapiro, who shared their anti-war sentiments but pointed out that for the famous and commercially successful artists among the AWC members, a call to boycott "the establishment" was hypocrisy: "A piece of self-righteous moralism that the community of protesting artists would find it hard to live up to in their own daily collaboration with museums, schools, galleries, and collectors."

If artists had to concede that conventional success could barely be achieved outside the art system, the system's institutions were also forced to acknowledge that the illusion of their neutrality had collapsed. For MoMA, the critical blow came from the publication of an article in *Art Forum* in June 1974 called "Abstract Expressionism, Weapon of the Cold War" by the artist and writer Eva Cockcroft, who outlined the links between senior MoMA personnel and the CIA. As part of its cultural mission against Soviet communism, the CIA had covertly funded some of the international exhibitions with which MoMA had so successfully promoted the "freedom and purity" of American abstract art. After this, no distinction between art and propaganda would ever seem simple.

The aesthetic criteria of the big museums were further attacked by artists such as Faith Ringgold (b. 1930). In 1968 and 1969 she led pickets against MoMA and the Whitney Museum of American Art for its exclusion of black and other minority artists from its major exhibitions. In 1970, with her daughter Michele Wallace, she formed Women Students and Artists for Black Art Liberation (WSABAL). Between 1963 and 1967 her series of paintings called *American People* had recorded the battles and wary truces which accompanied the Civil Rights movement and the rise of Black Power, a transition which saw the fight for legislated integration upstaged by militant separatism. *The Flag is Bleeding* (FIG. 86) shows her abil-

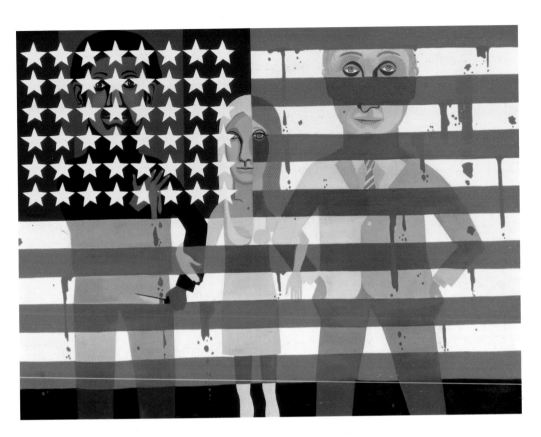

86. FAITH RINGGOLD
The Flag is Bleeding,
1967. Oil on canvas, 6′ x 8′
(1.82 x 2.43 m).

ity to invest a simple image with disturbing ambiguity. The flat, blandly coloured surface matches the inanely inexpressive faces of the white couple and black man who awkwardly pose arm-in-arm behind the veil of the national flag. The black man holds his right hand to his heart as if swearing allegiance or clutching a wound, while his other hand holds a small knife. Of the numerous protest images which featured the national flag, few registered so powerfully the extent to which it had lost its ability to function as a clear symbol, or certainly not one of national unity.

In 1967, the year the painting was made, the government sought to revive the annual Flag Day, 14 June, as a way, as Alabama Democrat Bill Nichols put it, of "showing heartfelt thanks to the United States soldiers fighting and dying for Old Glory in Vietnam." President Lyndon Johnson urged Americans to take up the flag on the day: "Fly it from your home, and from your place of business … and fly it in your heart." A week after Flag Day, Congress passed the federal flag desecration bill which toughened up prohibitions on expressions of disrespect for the flag. In 1970, Faith Ringgold was tried and convicted, along with Guerrilla Art Action Group campaigners Jean Toche and Jon Hendricks, for their event

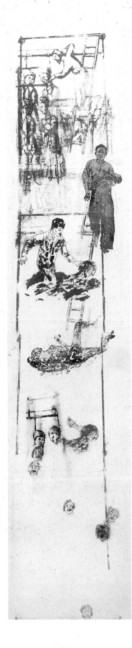

"The People's Flag Show" held in Judson Memorial Church to protest against the legislation. They stated: "If the flag can be used to sanctify killing, it should be available to people to stop killing." Among others charged were students at Hobart College, New York, who ended an anti-war play by washing the flag in a bathtub.

Nancy Spero's work has drawn together disparate images in order to uncover links between historical and contemporary forms of state violence, especially against women. During the Vietnam period she examined themes of war and sexual violence, and expanded these from the mid-1970s with visual and written studies based on Amnesty International's accounts of the torture of women in Latin America. In *Hanging Totem II* (1986; FIG. 87) she has combined pictures from an English sixteenth-century print recording witch hunts with images, like the woman carrying a child and the man dragging a woman by her hair, from the war in Vietnam. In 1984 Spero took part with hundreds of artists in the nationwide campaign Artists Call Against US Intervention in Central America, and with Josely Carvalho and other Latin American artists, helped organize an exhibition on the theme of *Rape and Intervention*. Carvalho has since developed these themes in art-works on the abuse of human rights in Latin America, and on the Gulf War (FIG. 88).

The Renewal of Dada

In Europe in the 1960s, traditions of committed realism, which had held sway as the mainstream art of the Left since the late nineteenth century, gave way to renewed interest in the alternative strategies of the historical avant-garde, particularly Dada. Dada, which had flourished only briefly as a protest movement during the First World War and its immediate aftermath, had established small groupings in Zurich, New York, Paris, Cologne, and Berlin. It was the German versions of Dada which had most forcefully insisted on its pacifist and anti-capitalist stance. The original German Dadaists had attempted to unify radical art-making with the revolutionary activism which broke out across Germany between 1919 and 1921. They had handed out their manifestos at factory gates and dodged the brutal *Freikorps* – right-wing vigilante gangs – in the streets of Berlin. Their critique of art took the form of challenging the privileged skill and "inspiration" of the artist and the elevation of the work of art to a precious object of reverence and material value. Their own "anti-art" works were deliberately cack-handed and disposable, or existed only as

87. NANCY SPERO
Hanging Totem II, 1986.
Zinc-cut stamps and zinc-cut stamp collage, 110 x 20" (274.5 x 52.1 cm).

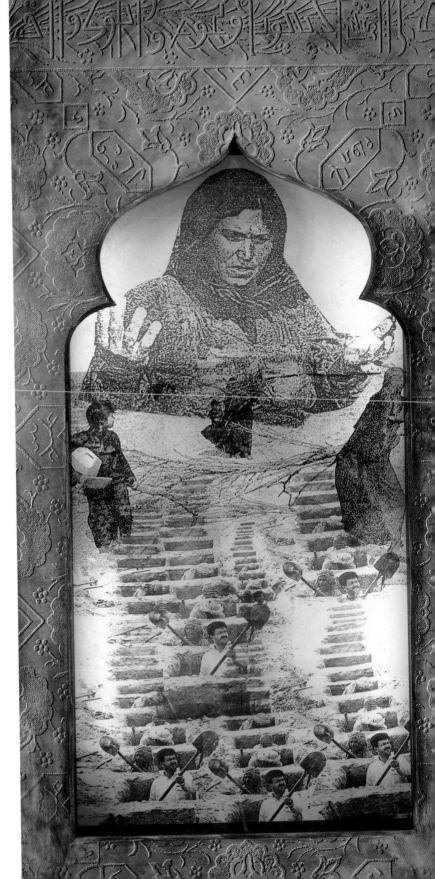

88. JOSELY CARVALHO
Basra, from installation
*It's Still Time to Mourn:
Dia Mater I,* 1993.
Silkscreen, wood, paper,
and lucite 56$\frac{1}{2}$ x 28$\frac{1}{2}$ x
9$\frac{3}{4}$″ (144 x 72 x 25 cm).
Collection of the artist.

confrontational actions. Their example struck a chord with political artists of the 1960s.

A large exhibition of Dada works held in Düsseldorf in 1958 helped to define the direction of the new emerging movement called Fluxus. Loosely structured, Fluxus was active in Europe and the United States during the 1960s. The most conspicuous and galvanizing personality among the artists was Joseph Beuys (1921-86), whose mixture of conviction, charisma, and showmanship held centre-stage among a new generation of radical German artists, who included Wolf Vostell (b. 1932), Gustav Metzger (b. 1926), K.P. Brehmer (b. 1938), Klaus Staeck (b. 1938), and Jörg Immendorff (b. 1945; FIG. 89). Beuys's work was firmly oriented towards performances, and the objects subsequently exhibited in galleries were often relics of these, the "props" transformed in the process of performance. In October 1972 he staged a boxing match "for direct democracy through referendum" (FIG. 90). This publicized and represented in dramatic form the campaign that he had led to reform electoral procedures and to introduce free admission to the Art Academy in Düsseldorf, where he was a professor of sculpture. Getting sacked from the Academy in the same year was also a kind of performance. The call for unlimited democracy and collective activity marked his political outlook: Everyone is an artist, he asserted, everyone who wants to learn is a student, and all social change must be creative.

89. JÖRG IMMENDORFF
Where do you Stand with your Art, Colleague? (Wo stehst du mit deiner Kunst, Kollege?), 1973. Diptych, synthetic resin on canvas, 4'3" x 6'11" (1.3 x 2.1 m).

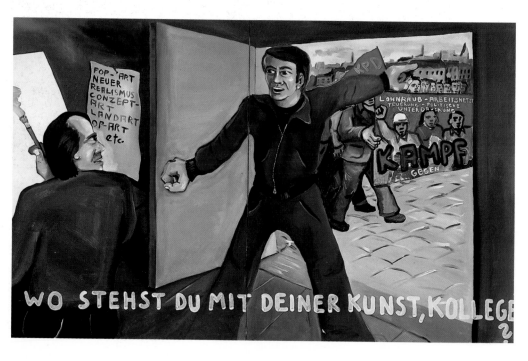

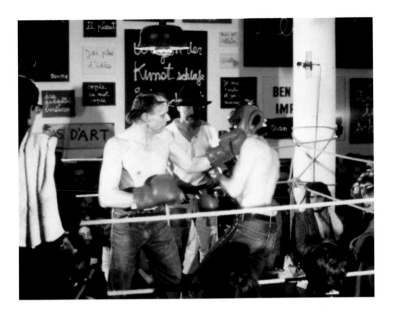

90. Joseph Beuys
*Boxing Match for Direct
Democracy through
Referendum*, 8 October
1972.

91. Wolf Vostell
Phänomene, 27 March 1965,
Berlin.

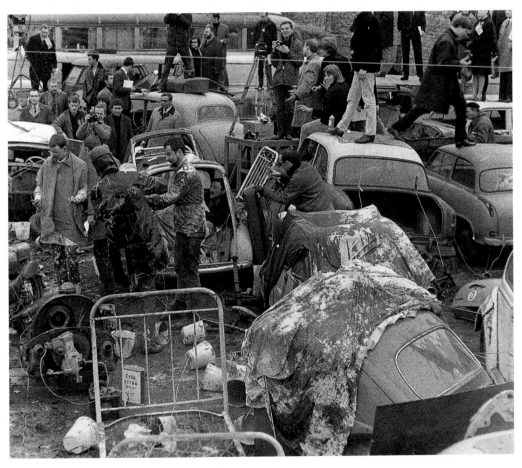

Beuys showed a remarkable capacity to carry others along with him; his students and fellow artists viewed him as a mentor and role-model. But the original Dadaists might well have regarded Beuys with mixed feelings. His egalitarian notion of art and his anti-didactic approach to teaching were at odds with his own cult status, carefully self-promoted, as the shaman-guru of radical art.

The Vietnam War cast its shadow over all the social concerns of European protest art in the 1960s and early 1970s. The German artist Wolf Vostell addressed the war repeatedly in his graphic works using altered or manipulated media pictures, and, impelled by Beuys's example and by American "Happenings," he arranged events like the 1965 *Phänomene* (FIG. 91). This congregation in a car dump involved the spontaneous contributions of poets, artists, and onlookers amidst the crumbling piles of broken cars (i.e., the detritus of capitalist production and destruction). This was, after all, the time when even a disorganized pop-concert like Woodstock was viewed as an experiment in alternative social gatherings, and a signifier of the new socio-political consciousness.

Paris '68

In France, the Vietnam War revived memories of French involvement in the war in Indo-China some ten years earlier, and the more recent colonial conflict in Algeria, which had provoked radical opposition from intellectuals, notably Jean-Paul Sartre (1905-80). Paris had long been a meeting place for black writers and artists from French colonies in Africa and the Caribbean. The city had been a centre for the growing cultural expression of Pan-Africanism and Black Consciousness movements since the 1920s. Against this background, the critique of colonialism and an awareness of Third World concerns were more developed in French intellectual life than in that of most other European countries. But the suddenness and vigour of the May Events in 1968 still came as a shock, probably even to those who took part in them. A series of minor clashes between students and police during the early weeks of May soon boiled over into a full-scale campaign of street battles. An eye-witness, Marc Rohan, recalled one of these off the Boulevard St Germain:

> For a few moments there was no possibility of retreat for the front ranks and we remained fully exposed to the truncheons and rifle butts. I was pushed onto the pavement in the crush and fell among some chairs stacked against the front

of a café. There I crouched, my arms protectively raised above my head, hearing the banging of truncheons against the metal of the chairs and occasionally feeling the blows reach me. Eventually, after what seemed like an awful long time, the marchers managed to turn back and retreat to the relative safety of the wide boulevard. There, instead of dispersing, they regrouped and faced the *gendarmes* again, this time to fight back.

Such actions mirrored those in major cities throughout Europe, and in their awareness of joining with the "moment" of '68, French students took up the chant: "Rome, Berlin, Madrid, Warsaw, PARIS." As if to confirm Che Guevara's "catalyst theory" of how a revolution could be sparked by minority insurgence, the student uprising galvanized a larger movement among factory workers towards a general strike, which ultimately involved some nine million people in numerous industries throughout France. Under the circumstances, there was relatively little bloodshed, though a schoolboy was drowned after a police beating on the banks of the Seine, and in June, two striking workers at the Sochaux Peugeot factory were shot dead by the CRS riot squad. Ending as abruptly as it had begun, the crisis was resolved by an emergency election in which the ruling party of Charles de Gaulle (1890-1970) easily defeated an unprepared and divided opposition.

The "cause" of the protesters covered a disparate cluster of local, national and international issues. This may explain both the breadth and intensity of dissent as well as the failure of their leaders to channel the radical impulse into a sustainable movement. Some of the students were motivated by practical demands for reform in the higher education system, which was overcrowded, underfunded, and fenced-in by forbidding entrance examination rules. Dissatisfaction with the conservative and remote style of teaching aggravated their view of the French establishment, and especially of the Gaullist government, as being authoritarian, inflexible, and out-dated. As the network of small "action committees" spread from the universities to factories, where plans of workers' control were drawn up, the radical student leaders viewed their struggle within a perspective of global revolution. They allied it to those of their heroes: Che Guevara in Cuba, Ho Chi Minh in Vietnam, and Mao Ze Dong in the People's Republic of China, although these revolutionary figures represented ideological positions which were quite distinct from each other. This perspective may not have helped to build common ground with the French factory workers nor with the "old" Communist Party of France (PCF). But for many involved, the rebellion may have been

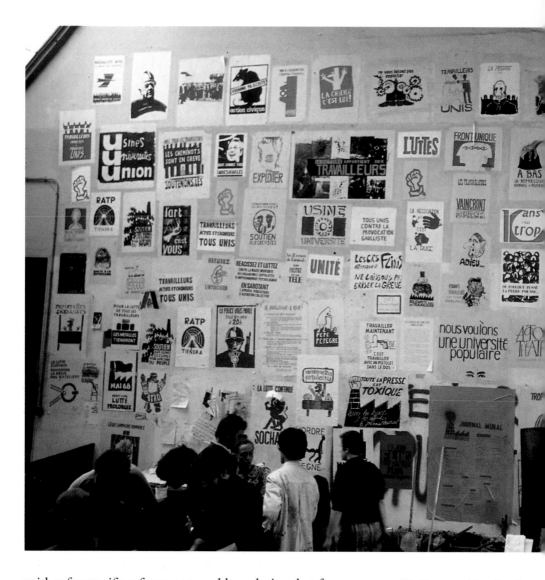

neither for specific reforms nor world revolution, but for a more general change of attitudes. These are reflected in the explosion of spontaneous graffiti and in the wit and immediacy of fly-poster and magazine graphics (FIGS 92 and 93) and youthful slogans: "Poetry is in the street ... Let us be realistic and demand the impossible ... Action must not be a reaction but a creation ... Speak to your neighbours ... Open the windows of your heart ... Run comrade, the world is behind you ... Love one another ... In any case, no regrets."

Though easily dismissed as naïve and hedonistic, the style of student dissent in the late 1960s was partly informed by beliefs which contrasted a notion of freedom in "play" with the commercialized

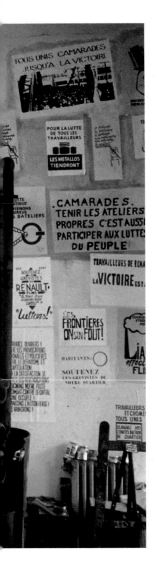

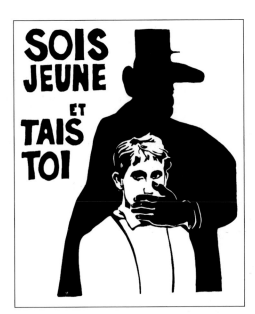

93. *Be Young and Shut Up* (Sois jeune et tais toi), May 1968, Paris. Poster.

forms of "pleasure" existing in what some French intellectuals, following the writings of Guy Debord (b. 1931), called "the society of the spectacle." In the 1920s, the Surrealists in France had applauded, as a political gesture, activities that were playfully absurd and purposeless, and therefore not harnessed to the utilitarian demands of the capitalist economy. This tradition was revived by the Situationist International, a group of artists and writers, including Debord, which formed in 1957, and reached its high point of relevance in May 1968. The Situationists drew on Marx's theory of "commodity fetishism," the condition under capitalism in which people are reduced to commodified objects by selling their labour, but shifted the emphasis from the effects of production to those of mass-consumption. They criticized the erosion of authentic social relations by the "spectacle" of mass-culture consumerism and its enforced habits of docile entertainment and empty pleasure.

These ideas were realized in the films and writings of a circle of *cinéastes* linked to the magazine *Les Cahiers du Cinéma*, and especially in the work of Jean-Luc Godard (b. 1930). The magazine had been co-founded in 1951 by the critic André Bazin (1918-58), who had called for a committed cinema based on realist principles. By using unobtrusive camera-angles and minimal editing, the conscientious film-maker should, in Bazin's view, seek to reveal everyday life with as much transparency and "truth" as possible. His ideals had been seen in the Italian neo-realism of the late 1940s, practised by directors like Roberto Rossellini (1906-77), and in France in the compassionate humanism of films by Robert Bresson (b. 1907). But after Bazin's death in 1958, the magazine voiced the values of a new wave of experimental directors, the most politically engaged of whom was Godard.

The contrast between Bazin's realism and Godard's avant-garde aesthetic was similar to the debate between Lukács and Brecht in the 1930s, discussed in Chapter One. Like Brecht, whom he greatly admired, Godard was concerned about the pacifying and manipulative effects of seductive illusions, exemplified in Hollywood movies. In his passionate love-hate view of Hollywood, he retained a belief in the power of cinema to reveal social truths, but deplored the glossy surface of the Hollywood style, and held that films, to be enlightening, must be critically "read." Godard's films use devices which deliberately remind the viewer of the artificial and "manufactured" nature of cinema. These devices

94. *Week-End,* directed by Jean-Luc Godard, 1968. Film still.

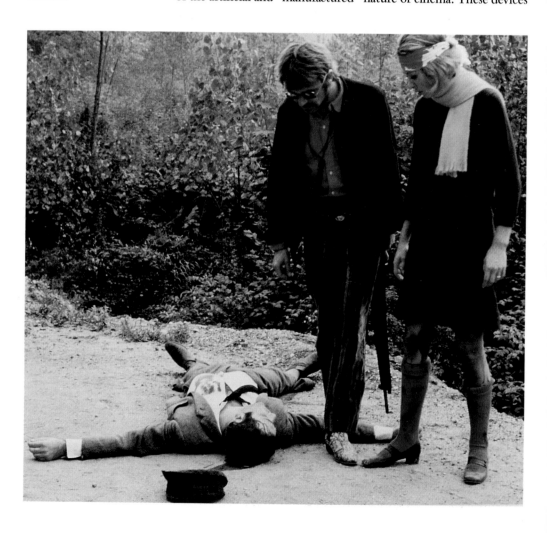

have included the jump-cut, which disrupts fluid editing, the dubbed soundtrack, which detaches sound from image, and the heightened use of primary colours. The narrative action may be interrupted by a character directly addressing the audience, or by a written text on the screen. The interweaving of emotional shocks with boredom, irritation, and unexpected comedy is also a strategy by which he has aimed to maintain in his audience a provoked, critical, and independent attitude. These effects are seen in his film *Week-End* (FIG. 94) in which modern society, explored in the appalling adventures of a middle-class couple on holiday in the French countryside, is depicted as a nightmare of greed, madness, random violence, car-crashes, and cannibalism. Typically, the film provides the audience with no simple guidance on how to respond to such scenes.

Before *Week-End*, Godard had worked on two films directly related to student protest and the Vietnam War, *La Chinoise* and the collectively made drama-documentary *Loin du Vietnam*, both of 1967. As well as other specific subjects, like the Algerian war and the Palestinian revolution, his films examine general conditions of work and sexual relationships. These are sometimes combined in the recurring topic of prostitution, which brings together themes of commercialized pleasure with commodified labour. The philosopher Gilles Deleuze (b. 1925), interviewed in *Les Cahiers du Cinéma* in 1976, referred to this when he said: "Godard asks very concrete questions; he shows images that relate to the following: What is it, in fact, that is bought, and what is sold? What is it that some people are prepared to buy and others to sell ...?" Godard claimed that his aim was "to make revolutionary films for revolutionary audiences." But although he has worked on television projects, and despite the frequent broadcasting of his major films, his uncompromising style has failed to appeal to a wide public. This raises the question: Can film-makers work outside (and against) the conventions of Hollywood-style entertainment, and still attract the viewing interests of cinema's large audiences?

Third Cinema: "The Camera is a Rifle"

This question has had a special relevance for film-makers in Third World countries, and particularly in those which have been shaped by European colonialism. Among Third World intellectuals who have argued that each colonized nation would need to forge its own independent culture in order to achieve real political and economic independence, Frantz Fanon (1925-61) has been an important figure. Born in Martinique, and trained as a psychiatrist, Fanon took part in Algeria's war of independence, and his book *The Wretched of the Earth* of 1961 became a key manifesto of anti-colonialism. He described colonialism as an experience which distorts the psychology of individual subjects, and argued that this can only be cured by a cultural renaissance. Fanon's ideas have been important for debates on the "de-colonization" of art and literature, and for the new approaches to film-making which flourished in Latin America in the 1960s, and in many different contexts in countries throughout Asia and Africa.

In Latin America, the development of radical approaches to film-making after the early 1960s had gained some support from the new revolutionary governments. In Cuba, soon after Fidel Castro came to power, the Cuban Institute of Film Art and Industry was set up to make documentaries and feature films which propagated the policies of the communist revolution. Havana also provided a place of refuge for film-makers in exile from Chile, where radical cinema had thrived after the election of Salvador Allende's Government of Popular Unity in 1970, until it was cut short by the military coup of 1973. Other expressions of new Latin American cinema had arisen in Brazil's Cinema Novo movement from the early 1960s, and the Documentary Film School of Santa Fe, Argentina, in the late 1950s. These had adapted the aesthetics of social documentary and Italian neo-realism to highlight the acute problems of poverty and inequality that were largely ignored by the mainstream film industry. The Brazilian director Glauber Rocha (1938-81) called this "The Aesthetics of Hunger."

The directors Octavio Getino and Fernando Solanas (b. 1936) of Argentina coined another important term in their manifesto *Towards a Third Cinema*. This was a rallying cry for an alternative to the first cinema, Hollywood, and the second cinema, European-influenced films made domestically. The founders of Third Cinema held a militant political perspective which viewed Hollywood as an instrument of imperialism, and saw alternative film-making as a weapon for transforming attitudes alongside armed revolution. The camera, they said, "is a rifle," the film is "a detonator," and the projector is "a gun that can shoot twenty-four frames per second." Exponents of Third Cinema held that it would not be enough just to change the content of films. The ways of telling a story and of depicting characters must also reflect local cultural traditions. Jorge Sanjinés (b. 1936) followed this principle in his *Blood of the Condor* (FIG. 95) which attacked the abuse of power by the US Peace Corps in Bolivia (it was based on evidence

95. *Blood of the Condor*, directed by Jorge Sanjinés, 1969. Film still.

of the forced sterilization of Indian peasants). Among Bolivia's Indian peasant communities, which make up some 65 per cent of the population, seeing a film was a rare or unknown experience. As well as involving villagers in making the film, Sanjinés tried new ways of showing it which adapted traditional modes of story-telling: "We had a narrator who first recounted the story by showing photographs of various characters. This is a tradition dating all the way back to the Incas and it still exists today – there are still story-tellers who journey from village to village. Then, afterwards, we discussed the story with the audience – and finally showed the film. It's a question of educating people unused to seeing movies at the same time as trying to create a national cinema."

The principles of Third Cinema have also been developed in Africa, where, for instance, the Senegalese director Ousmane Sembène (b. 1923) has been a leading practitioner. The self-educated son of a fisherman, he worked in France as a docker and trade union organizer, fought in the French colonial army in the Second World War, and became active in the French communist movement. In the 1960s, with a growing reputation as one of Africa's leading novelists, Sembène turned to film-making in order to reach a wider, non-literate audience. He studied the techniques of cinema at the Gorki Institute in Moscow, and his work shows an awareness of Italian neo-realism, Brechtian theatre and Soviet Marxist aesthetics. But his films absorb and reformulate these European approaches within a cinematic style which is embedded in African cultural traditions. He has used the themes and narrative structures of African folktales and parables, and incorporated songs, proverbs and oral history. He often described himself as a story-teller, or *griot*. The *griot* in West African societies was the village historian who recounted the community's past with a pointed critique of the present, acting as what Sembène calls "the living memory and conscience of his people": "The *griot* was not only the dynamic element of his tribe, clan and village, but also the authentic witness of each event. It was he who recorded and deposited before us, under the tree, the deeds and exploits of each person. The conception of my work is derived from this teaching: To remain as close as possible to reality and to the people."

Sembène made historical epics like *Emitai* (FIG. 96), which depicts a Senegalese rebellion against French colonial powers in the 1940s, and *Camp de Thiaroye* (1989), which tells the history of the mutiny and resulting massacre of African soldiers serving with the Free French Army in 1944. The excavation of colonial history has similarly been undertaken in the paintings of Senegalese artist Fodé Camara (b. 1958; FIG. 97) whose images of historical slavery also comment on the continuing abuse of human rights in modern Africa. Ousmane Sembène has also combined historical and contemporary themes directed against the black élites of post-colonial Senegal, where he sometimes faced government censorship. He has tackled a range of social issues: unemployment, foreign aid, corruption, polygamy, sexism, and religious intolerance. His film *Xala* (1974) is a livid comic satire of African middle-class morals. Its hero, a complacent businessman, is afflicted

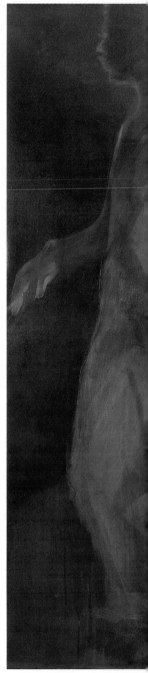

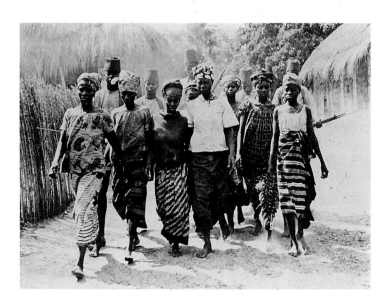

Left
96. *Emitai*, directed by Ousmane Sembène, 1971. Film still.

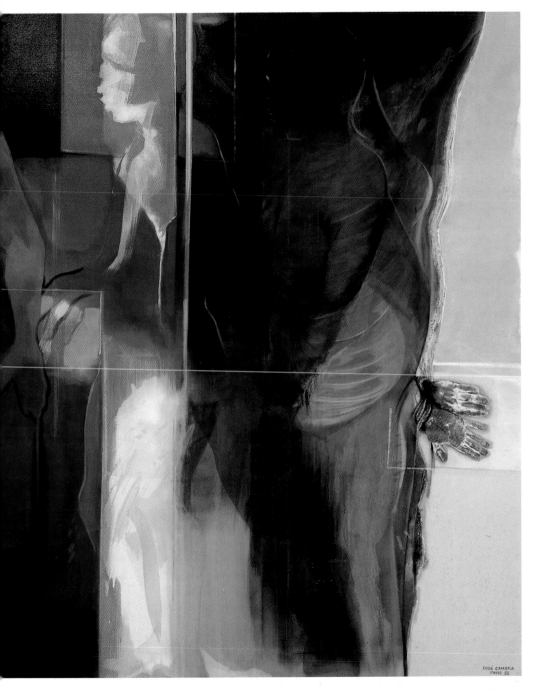

97. Fodé Camara
Passage I (Parcours I), 1988. Acrylic and pastel collage and
oil on canvas, 5′10⅞″ x 6′6¾″ (1.8 x 2 m). Fonds National
d'Art Contemporain, Paris.

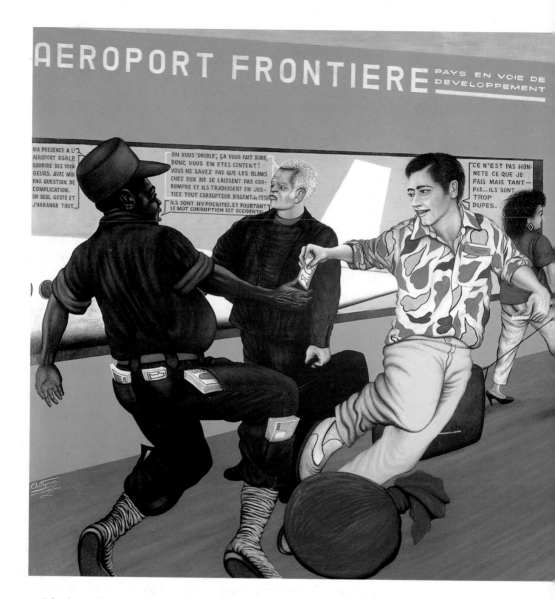

98. CHÉRI SAMBA
*Frontier Airport Country in
the Process of Development*
(Aéroport frontière pays en
voie de développement),
1990. Oil on canvas, 4'1" x
6'6¾" (1.5 x 2 m).

with the *xala*, an ancient curse which renders him impotent. His hapless search for a cure takes him through a social world which has been made equally impotent by self-serving bureaucracy and westernized affluence. For Sembène, who described cinema as "the night-school of the people," the involvement of the audience is vital. Unlike what he called socialist "poster films," his stories are often open-ended or provide several alternative endings. The outcomes and issues are to be worked out by the viewers, and he encouraged audience debates after screenings.

Of the very disparate kinds of recent political art in African countries, that of the painter Chéri Samba (b. 1956) is close in spirit

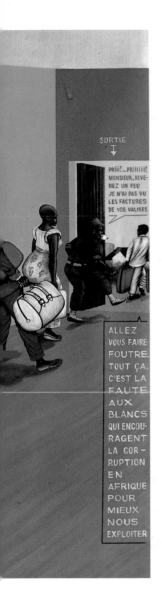

to Sembène's *griot* principles. Based in Kinshasa in Zaire, he initially trained as a sign-writer and also worked as a newspaper cartoonist. His paintings link closely to themes of satirical journalism and political caricatures, and draw on the narrative styles of advertising, television, and cinema. Their acidic colours match the biting wit with which he has attacked social and political vices. Selfish husbands, greedy politicians, randy schoolboys, and pimps populate his visual parables of human folly and injustice. A picture of an airport departure lounge (FIG. 98) shows a tourist casually handing a bribe to an African official while each privately criticizes the corruption of the other. From the late 1980s, Chéri Samba exhibited his work widely in Europe and the United States. As his pictures reached an international scene, his themes increasingly dealt with the dark side of relationships between Africa and the West.

Feminism(s)

Launched amidst the Civil Rights movements of the late 1960s, modern feminism, in its many forms, has gradually made a deep impact on mainstream art practices and the academic world. In a microcosm, this condition was rehearsed by a small group of art students and their tutors in an experimental course called the Feminist Art Program at Fresno State College, California, which began in 1970 and was the model for a subsequent programme at California Institute of the Arts in 1971. Fresno State College had been a site of political turmoil: Five teachers had been fired for radical activism, but students and faculty had set up courses in Marxism, Anarchist theory and Black, Chicano and Armenian studies. The Los Angeles sculptor Judy Chicago (b. 1939) was appointed to head the new Feminist Art Program. She took the course off-campus and set up studios in a former barracks. Here Chicago and her students tried out a range of activities which anticipated the main approaches of future feminist art: working collectively; exploring the history and cultural representation of women; exploding dominant stereotypes in pictures, performances, and installations; and combining highly-charged sessions of personal discussion with public agitational events. Under Chicago's charismatic leadership, the students were encouraged to "up-front" their sexuality in "consciousness-raising" seminars, looking for more assertive ways of representing sexuality and confronting what they viewed as the phallocentric imagery of the patriarchal order. A conspicuous theme in their work was the elaboration of the most taboo marker of femininity by making what the

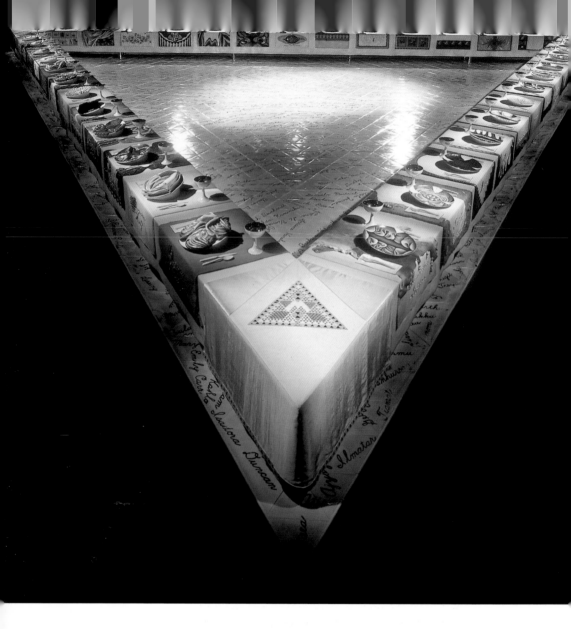

99. JUDY CHICAGO
The Dinner Party, 1974–78. Multimedia installation, 48' x 48' x 48'
(1.463 x 1.463 x 1.463 m).

The Dinner Party marked the achievements of women in history. As
Judy Chicago explained: "From my studies of women's art and
literature and my research into women's lives – undertaken as part of
my search for my own tradition as a woman and an artist – I had
concluded that the general lack of knowledge of our heritage as
women was pivotal in our continued oppression. It caused us all to
have an unconsciously diminished feeling of self-worth and lack of
pride in women."

students cheerfully called "cunt art." Faith Wilding recalled, "We vied with each other to come up with images of female sexual organs by making paintings, drawings, and constructions of bleeding slits, holes and gashes, boxes, caves, or exquisite vulval jewel boxes. Making 'cunt art' was exciting, subversive, and fun, because 'cunt' signified to us an awakening consciousness about our bodies and our sexual selves." Chicago drew together many of these early approaches in her famous project *The Dinner Party* (FIG. 99), begun in 1974 and finished with the help of a large group of volunteer assistants in 1978 when it opened at the San Francisco Museum of Modern Art to near record-breaking crowds. Consisting of a triangular arrangement of tables, each 48 feet long, the piece evoked a gathering of notable women from history and mythology. Each of the 39 place settings had a specially designed plate, decorated with a womb-like or "central core" motif, a cup, and an embroidered cloth runner. On the floor, the names of a further 900 women distinguished in history were written on marble tiles. Its effect combined domesticity with an atmosphere of communion. Chicago explained that her aim had been to help generate a sense of women's unrecognized heritage and achievement: "Because we were educated to think that women had never achieved anything of significance, it was easy to believe that we we're incapable of ever accomplishing important work." The piece helped to stimulate new approaches to monumental art which sought to recover textile design and decorative crafts from their low status in the conventional art world.

As in the anti-war demonstrations, American feminist activism in the late 1960s and 1970s readily blended "artistic" performance with the impromptu styles of street protest, seen for example in the 1968 disruption of the Miss America Pageant in Atlantic City and the actions of WITCH (Women's International Terrorist Conspiracy from Hell). The criticism of media images of women and the aim to create alternative imagery was a priority for the women's movement in general, and not just a concern of its artistic wing. Among many alliances, performance artists Leslie Labowitz and Suzanne Lacey worked closely with campaign groups such as Women Against Violence Against Women (WAVAW) and Rape Crisis Hotlines to produce, in 1977, the collective event *In Mourning and in Rage* at Los Angeles City Hall. This commemorated the victims of sexual murders and protested against the exploitative treatment of them in the press. On the East Coast, Mary Beth Edelson, who was aligned to the Women's Spirituality Movement, performed rituals in urban and natural settings devoted to goddess worship and witchcraft. Some are recorded

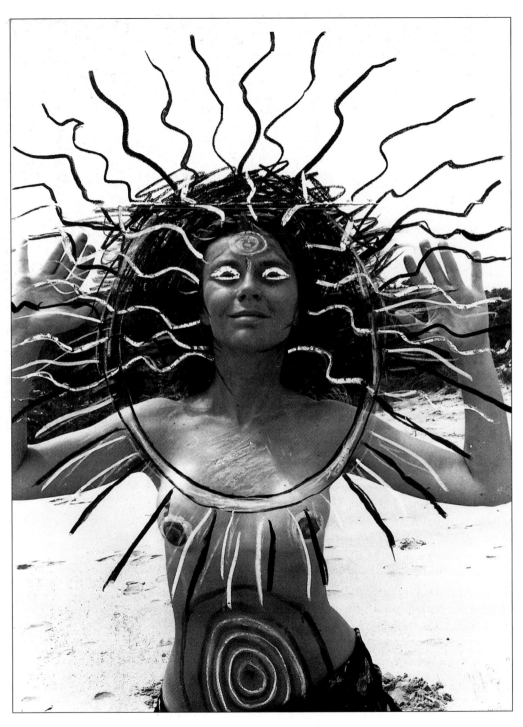

100. MARY BETH EDELSON
Woman Rising with Spirit, 1974. Performance on the Outter
Banks, North Carolina, U.S.A. Photograph with drawing.

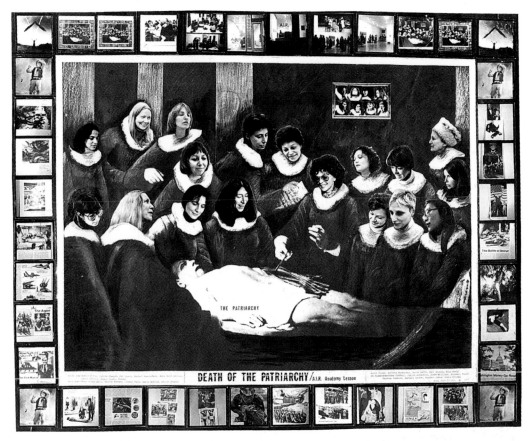

DEATH OF THE PATRIARCHY/A.I.R. Anatomy Lesson

in the photographic series *Woman Rising* (FIG. 100). As well as founding an all-women gallery in New York, Edelson set up performance workshops which, like many other feminist art activities, brought together professional and amateur artists. Her *Death of the Patriarchy* (FIG. 101) transforms Rembrandt's *The Anatomy Lesson of Dr. Tulp* (1632) into a triumphant image of feminist artists dismembering a male-dominated discourse. The old communist-aligned avant-garde groups of the 1920s and 1930s, like the German Dadaists and the Surrealists in France, had never achieved this creative relationship with their wider political movement. Feminism in the 1970s helped to open up the narrow professional control of galleries, and broadened the range of art journals. It also had a profound effect on academic art history, jolting the discipline out of its connoisseurial reverence for the "great masters."

As feminism developed in the 1980s, sexual difference was increasingly interpreted as socially constructed. This contrasted with earlier conceptions of femininity which tended to view it as a universal and biologically determined essence. The non-essentialist view enabled the movement to link its concerns with

101. MARY BETH EDELSON
Death of the Patriarchy/
A.I.R. Anatomy Lesson,
1976. Offset poster.

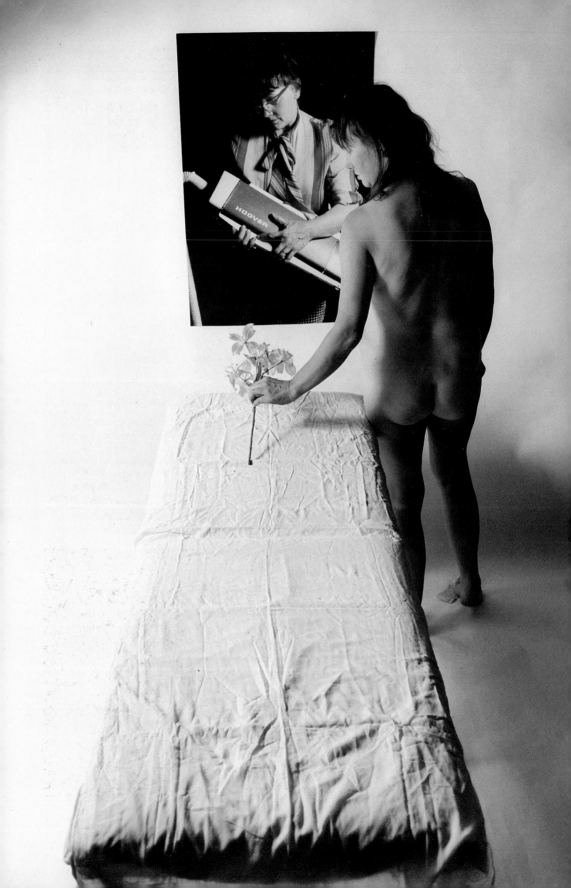

other kinds of difference, like those of class and race. While the notion that "the personal is political" had been a famous slogan in the late 1960s, by the 1980s it was the premise for a theoretical pursuit of an amalgamation of Marxist social theories with psychoanalytical accounts of the formation of subjectivity. Of these, the writings of Jacques Lacan (1901-81) and Julia Kristeva (b. 1941) about the socialization of the growing infant through its access to language were particularly influential. These ideas intersected, for example, in the photographic work of British artist Jo Spence (1934-92) who, after leaving school at the age of thirteen and working as a wedding and portrait photographer, became involved with left-wing groups and the innovative magazine *Camerawork*. She gradually rejected the realist conventions of social documentary and began to write about popular forms of self-representation in the snapshots of family albums. From 1982 she recorded in photographs her struggle against breast cancer and against the medical establishment; she refused to have a mastectomy and made photographs which angrily parodied the medical world's view of her body as an object of institutional knowledge and power. This led her towards a form of phototherapy in which she explored the history of her life by re-creating in self-portraits the stereotypes which had shaped her sense of identity as a working-class woman. The ways in which she depicts her recollections of the views that she had of herself as an adolescent are often wickedly funny. A more painful recurring theme was the mixture of shame and guilt with which she had viewed her uneducated mother, and she explored this in staged photographs as a way to understand and come to terms with the distortion of the inner life by attitudes of class and gender (FIG. 102). Un-

Opposite
102. JO SPENCE IN COLLABORATION WITH DAVID ROBERTS
Untitled photograph, 1989. Jo Spence Memorial Archive, London.

103. MONA HATOUM *Measures of Distance*, 1988. Colour video still. Mona Hatoum.

til her death in 1992, she worked on projects to encourage phototherapy groups for working-class women.

The Palestinian artist Mona Hatoum, who left Beirut to live in London in 1975, became widely known after a series of performances and installations made during the civil war in Lebanon. Like Jo Spence, she acts out inner dramas of her personal history that express political concerns of alienation and division (FIG. 103). Her performances often set up an

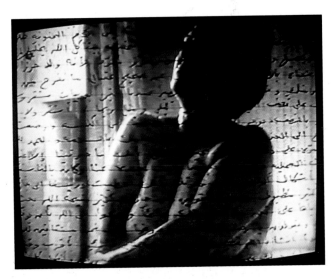

intimate proximity with an audience, but also feature claustro-phobic devices of separation: She has shown herself confined in a cage-like structure, a transparent box, and wrapped in a hood or veil. These barriers restrict both physical movement and com-munication, and express the wider condition of being separated from a nation which itself has been colonized and divided. The allusions to imprisonment also evoke the way the foreign cul-ture to which she is exiled will continually try to restrict her to the position of an outsider. The work of Spence and Hatoum is characteristic of the kind of art in which there is no fixed distinction between self-expression and political statement.

Propaganda Against Propaganda

The 1980s and 1990s saw a widening diversity in approaches to political art, many of which achieved a high profile in the art scenes

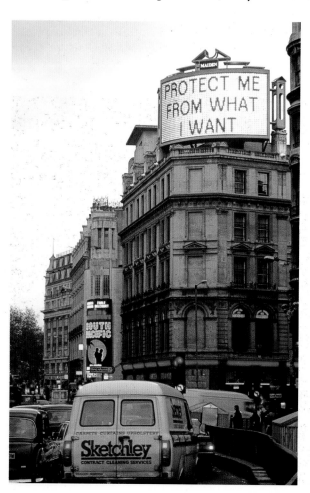

104. JENNY HOLZER
Protect Me from What I Want Work in Picadilly Circus, London, 1988. Electronic signboard.

of the United States and Western Europe. In the expanding art cen-tres of New York and Los Ange-les, the effects of the AIDS epidemic and the conservatism of the Reagan-Bush administrations provoked polit-ical engagement among a new post-Vietnam generation of artists, critics and curators. But at the same time, and as the traditional concerns of the Left began to fragment, the idea of conveying a political "message" became increasingly problematic. A concept of "revolutionary art" now seemed anachronistic; Marx's prediction of the imminent collapse of capitalism had apparently died in the wake of 1968, and the experi-ments of the communist states which fell apart in the late 1980s were conclusively discredited. A body of theories linked to the notion of postmodernism identified the strengthening of multinational capi-talist power by its dispersal across the information systems of global TV and computer networks. Some spoke of the loss of the "real" world and its substitution by a realm of simulations. The political artist faced the task of finding a means of expression in the midst of a superabundance of messages.

The text-based work of the American artist Jenny Holzer (b. 1950) encourages a suspicion of verbal messages, and especially of didactic or opinionated statements. On posters, bronze plaques, engraved granite slabs, and electronic sign-boards, Holzer writes messages which are not in "her" voice, but in styles that mimic the anonymous voices of authority: government, education, advertising, and other, sometimes undefinable, sources of public advice or private confession (FIG. 104). Among her early projects was the series of posters called *Truisms*, which first appeared on the walls of streets in Lower Manhattan in 1977. With no accompanying images, these simply listed hundreds of statements in alphabetical order. The statements assumed various manners of speech, such as instructions, slogans, platitudes, rebukes, and demands: A POSITIVE ATTITUDE MAKES ALL THE DIFFERENCE IN THE WORLD; DON'T RUN PEOPLE'S LIVES FOR THEM; HIDING YOUR MOTIVES IS DESPICABLE; REMEMBER YOU ALWAYS HAVE FREEDOM OF CHOICE. Individually, each statement may be convincing or persuasive, but

105. JENNY HOLZER *Under a Rock*, 1986–89. Installation with granite benches and LED (light-emitting diode screens). Installed at Barbara Gladstone Gallery, New York.

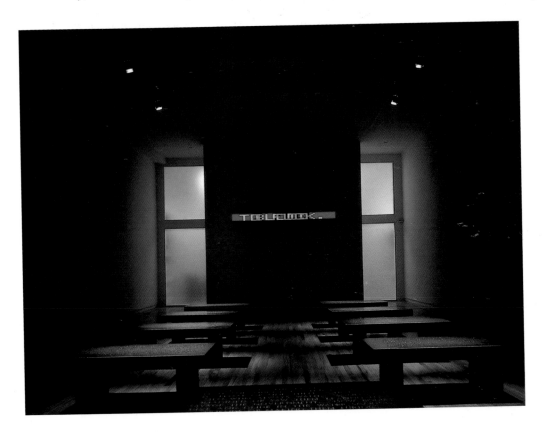

as they accumulate, they begin to set up contradictions and start to cancel each other out. Holzer's use of reiteration bombards the viewer with an overload of opinions, which, like so many propaganda messages, evince certainty without sincerity. By placing these in urban settings, alongside real advertisements, street signs, and traffic signals, she reflects the experience of city life in which the proliferation of competing messages has created a bewildering forest of authoritarian signs. In museum settings, her installations create an atmosphere which makes the museum environment seem like an ominous place of obscure instruction (FIG. 105). Describing Holzer's work, the critic Hal Foster (b. 1955) wrote: "Coercive languages are usually hidden, at work everywhere and nowhere: When they are exposed they look ridiculous. And the Truisms do read like a dictionary of such languages, with the effect that they are depleted, robbed of their 'fascist' power."

Also concerned with the effects and limits of language, Rita Donagh has, since the 1970s, worked on pictures about the conflict in Northern Ireland. These do not take sides; instead they use reticence and ambiguity to investigate the inability of words

106. Republican mural, Belfast, Northern Ireland.

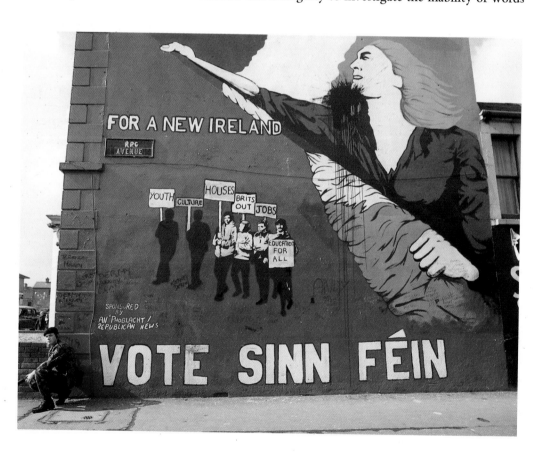

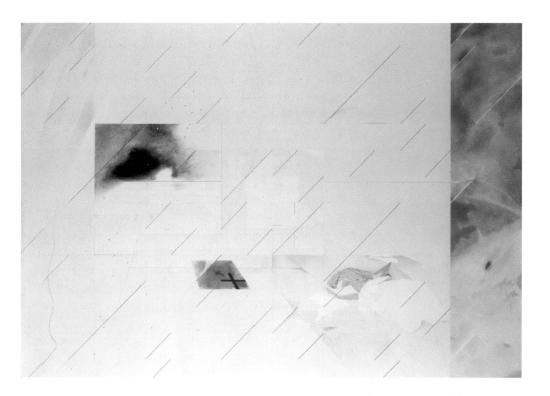

and images to reveal adequately the complex and ultimately invisible situation known as "the Troubles." The political culture of Northern Ireland has been marked by the over-production of slogans and symbols: Both Loyalists and Republicans use street murals, uniformed marching bands, and quasi-religious parades to maintain the territorial presence of their competing iconographies (FIG. 106). Both sides have staged terrorist acts for the press and television. In 1988 the British government imposed a temporary ban on broadcasting the voices of paramilitary members on radio and television to deny them, as Margaret Thatcher put it, "the oxygen of publicity." This suffocating atmosphere is conveyed in Donagh's paintings. *Evening Papers (Ulster 1972-74)* (FIG. 107) shows her painstaking method of building up thin layers of paint and oblique faint lines to suggest the mental after-images of urban landscapes, maps, and TV pictures. The small veiled shape to the lower-right was taken from a *Sunday Times* photograph of the body of a man killed by a car-bombing in Talbot Street, Dublin, in 1974. His body was covered with newspapers. With this image Donagh contrasts the reality of death with its "coverage" in words and pictures. Conveying no simple message, her decentred compositions imply only a sense of the difficulty of finding a "position" from which to view, speak, or act.

107. RITA DONAGH *Evening Papers (Ulster 1972–74)*, 1973–74. Oil, pencil, and collage on canvas, 4'7" x 6'7" (1.4 x 2 m). The British Council, London.

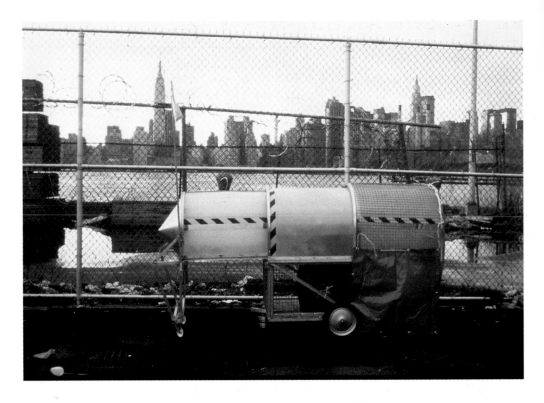

108. Krzysztof Wodiczko
Homeless Vehicle, 1988.
Aluminium, steel mesh,
plexiglas, and off the shelf
wheels.

Against Silence and Invisibility

Jenny Holzer and Rita Donagh, among many artists of the 1980s
and 1990s, have produced work which addresses the problems
of representation in the media-saturated environment of contemporary life. Holzer draws attention to the exercise of authority which underlies the verbal message. Donagh shows how a political situation is concealed behind symbols, and how media
representations of death erase access to meaning and emotional
response. The problems of representation have also been unrav-
elled in debates about what has been called the construction of
"otherness." This concerns ways in which certain groups are
subject to representation in a manner which serves to marginal-
ize them as "other" to an implicit normality. This effect was
discussed in Chapter One in relation to Lewis Hine's photographs
of New York's poor at the turn of the century, in which, though
benign in intention, he rendered his subjects as the passive recip-
ients of middle-class benevolence. Jo Spence complained about
similar effects in aid charities' depictions of Third World poverty
through photographs of starving children which reiterate a view
of "the poor abroad" as underdeveloped, silent, and powerless (and
therefore unthreatening) in relation to the charitable values of the

West. Those artists who wish to be of service to a marginalized group risk what the writer Craig Owens referred to as "the indignity of speaking for others."

One possible way to evade this problem was posited by the artist Krzysztof Wodiczko (b. 1943) in his work on New York homelessness, in which he sought to replace the use of images with the production of a functioning object in his Homeless Vehicle Project, developed in the late 1980s (FIG. 108). Wodiczko described the homeless as "exiles in their own city." Rendered invisible by passers-by who ignore them, "they are reduced to mere observers of the remaking of their neighborhoods for others. Their homelessness appears as a natural condition, the cause is dissociated from its consequence, and the status of the homeless as legitimate members of the urban community is unrecognized." Working with designers, and consulting with a team of homeless people, Wodiczko identified as a central requirement of homeless survival the improvised vehicles, often shopping and postal carts, used to carry belongings and to store recyclable refuse. The team worked on designing a purpose-built vehicle, producing a prototype which incorporated an insulated sleeping space, washing basin, toilet, and storage for collected goods. They also developed the provision of locks, alarm system, and the means to join together the vehicles to form small hamlets for added safety. While aiming to provide a life-saving object, the project was not without an element of propaganda; as Wodiczko stressed, "the signifying function of the vehicle is as important as its strictly utilitarian purpose." In use, the vehicle would reveal the active involvement of the homeless with the economy of the city where "their visibly purposive movement through the city gives them an identity as actors in the urban space." A two-way message, this "signifying function" might "build a bridge of empathy between homeless people and observers."

The struggle against silence and invisibility was, for many, a matter of life and death in the face of the AIDS epidemic from the early 1980s. For gay communities, in particular, this meant defending and cherishing the human face of victims of the disease against an onslaught, most virulent in the early years, of media and government representations which were all too often moralistic and vindictive. Gay activist groups like ACT UP, Gran Fury, and Art+Positive used guerrilla tactics, like fly-posting the streets, and also commissioned advertisements and billboards to spread the counter-message. "Silence=Death" and "All People with AIDS are Innocent" were among slogans which fought their way into the public domain. The inadequacy of early official

109. CLEVE JONES (originator)
The NAMES Project AIDS Memorial Quilt (overview), 1985–present. Fabric, each panel, 36 x 72" (91 x 182 cm).

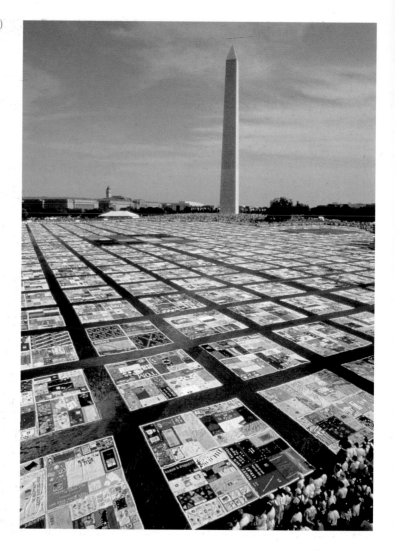

responses to the disease – the failure, for example, of government education to explain the ins and outs of safe sex for the sake of "decency" – brought the body, sexuality, and the definition of "obscenity" to the forefront of concerns in political art. The Christian Right, especially in America, raged back with equal force. In the midst of the fury was the search for the means to commemorate and grieve for the dead. The most successful and well known of memorials has been the AIDS Quilt, coordinated by The NAMES Project, a San Francisco-based volunteer group supported by private donations (FIGS 109 and 110). The quilt was first shown in Washington during the 1987 National March for Gay and Lesbian Rights. Each three by six-foot panel is sewn by the lovers, friends, and family of someone who has died of

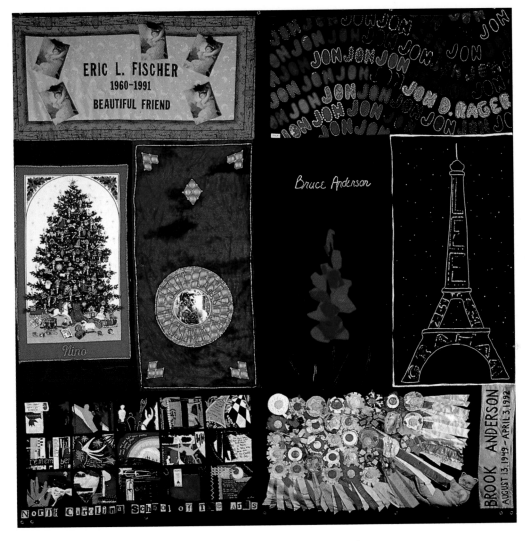

AIDS-related illness, and decorated with names, messages, pictures, mementos, a piece of clothing or a gift. The panels are laced together and publicly shown, though there are now so many that only a part of it can be gathered in any one space. Speaking many voices, existing in no single place, movable, expandable, made both privately and collectively, and able to remember an individual within an inclusive community, the quilt may have succeeded in bringing together the political and human functions of art.

110. *The NAMES Project AIDS Memorial Quilt* (detail), 1985–present. Fabric, each panel, 36 x 72″ (91 x 182 cm).

Political events | Science and technolo

1900-1910

	Political events		Science and technolo
1900	The Boxer rising in China	**1900**	First flight of Zeppelin airship
1900	The first Pan-African Conference	**1901**	First trans-Atlantic radio transmission
1901	US President McKinley assassinated		Morse code
1902	The Boer War in South Africa ends	**1903**	Flight of the Wright brothers
1905	Failed revolution in Russia	**1904**	New York subway opens
1906	Leon Trotsky is exiled to Siberia	**1907**	Ivan Pavlov publishes *Conditioned Re*
1907	Revolutions in Argentina and Nicaragua	**1908**	H. Geiger invents the Geiger counter
1908	Austria annexes Bosnia and Herzegovina	**1910**	Marie Curie publishes *Treatise on*
1909	Execution of Spanish anarchist Francisco Ferrer		*Radiography*
1910	The Mexican Revolution		

1911-1920

1911	Revolution in China	**1912**	The Vickers machine gun introduced
1912	Woodrow Wilson elected US president		British army
1914	The First World War begins	**1913**	The Model-T Ford in mass-production
1914	The Battle of Mons	**1914**	The Panama Canal opens
1915–16	The Gallipoli Campaign	**1915**	Poison gas first used at Ypres
1916	The Somme Offensive	**1916**	First use of the military tank in France
1917	USA enters the First World War	**1917**	Clarence Birdseye develops frozen foo
1917	The October Revolution, Russia		storage
1919	The Treaty of Versailles	**1920**	J.T. Thompson invents the sub-machir
1919	Communist uprising in Germany		gun

1921-1930

1922	Mussolini gains power in Italy	**1921**	First medium-wave broadcast in the U
1923	Calvin Coolidge elected US President	**1922**	Alexander Graham Bell dies
1923	The Republic of Turkey is formed under Mustafa Kemal	**1925**	John Scopes is tried in Tennesse for te
1923	Hitler is imprisoned after the Munich Putsch		Darwinism
1924	Lenin dies	**1926**	T. H. Morgan publishes *The Theory of*
1926	General Strike in Britain		*Gene*
1927	Trotsky is expelled from the Soviet Communist Party	**1928**	Alexander Fleming discovers penicillii
1928	The First Five-Year Plan is launched in USSR	**1928**	Colour television is developed in Brita
1928	The Guomindang nationalists capture Beijing	**1929**	The Kodak company develop 16mm o
1929	The Wall Street Crash		film

1931-1940

1931	Japanese army occupies Manchuria	**1932**	Karl Jansky develops radio astronomy
1932	The Indian National Congress is banned in India	**1932**	James Chadwick discovers the Neutro
1933	Hitler becomes Chancellor in Germany	**1933**	Ernst Ruska builds an electron microsc
1933	US President Roosevelt introduces the New Deal	**1935**	Radar developed in Britain
1934	César Sandino is murdered by the Nicaraguan	**1937**	First jet engine is built in Britain
	National Guard	**1938**	Introduction of fibreglass and teflon
1936	The Spanish Civil War begins	**1939**	German physicists achieve nuclear fis
1936	The British Union of Fascists march in London	**1939**	Pan-American Airways begin regular
1938	The Moscow Trials continue, Bukharin is shot for treason		Atlantic flights
1939	Germany annexes Czechoslovakia and invades Poland		
1940	Germany invades Denmark, Norway, Holland, and France		

1941-1950

1941	Germany invades the Soviet Union	**1941**	Manhattan Project for atomic bomb
1941	Japan attacks Pearl Harbor		research begins
1944	Allied forces land in Normandy	**1942**	First V2 rocket is launched in German
1945	Atomic bombing of Hiroshima and Nagasaki	**1944**	Invention of the kidney machine,
1945	Germany and Japan surrender		Netherlands
1946	Winston Churchill coins the term "iron curtain"	**1946**	The Soviet Union starts its first nuclear
1947	Announcement of the Truman Doctrine and Marshall		reactor
	Plan	**1947**	First supersonic air flight by a US plane
1948	Apartheid begins in South Africa	**1947**	Invention of holograms
1949	NATO is founded	**1947**	Microwave ovens go on sale
1950	The Korean War begins	**1952**	USA explodes the first hydrogen bomb

Other cultural events	Visual arts

00	Sigmund Freud's *The Interpretation of Dreams*	1901	Picasso's first exhibition in Paris
02	Enrico Caruso's first recording	1903	Paul Gauguin dies
03	Edwin Porter's film *The Great Train Robbery*	1904	Giacoma Balla's painting *A Worker's Day*
04	Joseph Conrad's novel *Nostromo*	1905	Die Brücke formed in Dresden
06	The Biograph film studio opens in New York	1907	Picasso's *Les Desmoiselles d'Avignon*
08	Jack Johnson wins world heavyweight title	1908	Constantin Brancusi's sculpture *The Kiss*
07	J.M. Singe's play *Playboy of the Western World*	1908	Wilhelm Worringer publishes *Abstraction and Empathy*
10	Leo Tolstoy dies	1909	F.T. Marinetti's *The Foundation and Manifesto of Futurism*

12	The US Modesty League campaigns against tight dresses	1912	Guillaume Apollinaire publishes *The Cubist Painters*
13	Igor Stravinsky's ballet *The Rite of Spring*	1913	Marcel Duchamp's ready-made sculpture *Bicycle Wheel*
13	D.H. Lawrence's novel *Sons and Lovers*	1913	The Armory Show, New York
15	D.W. Griffith's film *Birth of a Nation*	1915	The 0.10 exhibition, Petrograd
15	Charlie Chaplin's film *The Tramp*	1916	The Cabaret Voltaire opens in Zurich
17	The Death of Buffalo Bill Cody	1917	De Stijl is formed in Leyden
18	Oswald Spengler publishes *The Decline of the West*	1918	The Novembergruppe is formed in Germany
19	Robert Weine's film *The Cabinet of Dr. Caligari*	1919	The Bauhaus is founded in Weimar
		1920	Naum Gabo makes *Kinetic Construction*

21	Rudolph Valentino stars in *The Sheik*	1920	Le Corbusier and A. Ozanfant publish *Purism*
22	The BBC is formed	1922	Joan Miró's painting *The Farm*
22	Robert Flaherty's documentary *Nanook of the North*	1923	El Lissitzky's installation *Proun Room*
22	T.S. Eliot's *The Wasteland*	1924	André Breton publishes *The first Manifesto of Surrealism*
22	Ludwig Wittgenstein's *Tractatus Logico-Philosophicus*	1924	Leon Trotsky publishes *Literature and Revolution*
26	Ernest Hemingway's novel *The Sun Also Rises*	1926	Claude Monet dies
27	First full-length talkie *The Jazz Singer*	1929	The Museum of Modern Art, New York, founded
30	The Hays Code for Hollywood film censorship is introduced	1929	Salvador Dali joins the Surrealist group
30	Russian poet Vladimir Mayakovsky commits suicide	1930	Thomas Hart Benton begins *City Scenes* murals, New York
		1930	Grant Wood exhibits *American Gothic*

		1932	The John Reed Club of New York publishes its *Draft Manifesto*
31	James Cagney stars in *The Public Enemy*	1931–32	Ben Shahn paints *Sacco and Vanzetti*
34	Jean Vigo's film *L'Atalante*	1932	Independent art groups are banned in the Soviet Union
33	George Orwell publishes *Down and Out in Paris and London*	1933	The Bauhaus is closed
34	The First Congress of Soviet Writers	1935	The Federal Arts Project is introduced in the United States
35	Jazz is banned in German radio	1936	The Cubism and Abstract Art exhibition, New York
36	James Cain's novel *Double Indemnity*	1937	Picasso's painting *Guernica*
36	The 11th Olympic Games are held in Berlin	1939	Renato Guttusso's painting *Flight from Etna*
37	Walt Disney's film *Snow White and the Seven Dwarfs*	1939	Clement Greenberg publishes *Avant-Garde and Kitsch*
40	Carl Jung publishes *Psychology and Religion*	1940	David Siqueiros is implicated in the assassination of Trotsky
40	German writer Walter Benjamin commits suicide		

41	Humphrey Bogart stars in *The Maltese Falcon*	1941	Adolph Gottlieb begins his series of *Pictographs*
41	Richard Wright's novel *Native Son*	1941	The Mount Rushmore Memorial is completed
42	Albert Camus's novel *The Outsider*	1943	Arshile Gorky's painting *Waterfall*
45	Alfred Hitchcock's film *Spellbound*	1944	Edvard Munch dies
46	Jean-Paul Sartre publishes *Existentialism and Humanism*	1945	Boris Taslitsky's painting *The Small Camp at Buchenwald*
48	Antonio Gramsci publishes *Prison Notebooks*	1947	Alberto Giacometti's sculpture *Man Pointing*
50	Arthur M. Schlesinger Jr publishes *The Politics of Freedom*	1947	Eduardo Paolozzi's collage *I Was a Rich Man's Plaything*
50	Billy Wilder's film *Sunset Boulevard*	1948	COBRA forms, Paris
		1950	Jackson Pollock's painting *Autumn Rhythm*
		1950	Willem de Kooning's painting *Excavation*

	Political events	Science and technolo|gy

<table>
<tr><td rowspan="1">1951-1960</td>
<td>
1952 Coronation of Queen Elizabeth II
1952 The Mau Mau fight British rule in Kenya
1953 Stalin dies
1954 General Nasser becomes prime minister of Egypt
1956 Fidel Castro and his guerrilla forces land in Cuba
1956 Nikita Khrushchev denounces Stalin
1956 Britain clashes with Egypt in Suez Crisis
1958 Charles de Gaulle elected French president
1960 South African police kill 69 at the Sharpeville massacre
</td>
<td>
1954 First flight of the US Boeing 707
1954 Launch of the first nuclear submarine
1957 Soviet Union launches two Sputnik satellite
1958 USA launches five satellites and a rocket
1959 Britain launches the Mini Minor
1960 The contraceptive pill is widely available in USA
</td></tr>

<tr><td>1961-1970</td>
<td>
1961 US-backed invasion of Cuba fails at the Bay of Pigs
1962 Cuban missile crisis
1963 J.F. Kennedy is assassinated in Dallas, Texas
1965 Malcolm X is assassinated in Manhattan, New York
1965 USA begins regular bombing in North Vietnam
1966 China's Cultural Revolution begins
1967 The Six Day War between Israel and Egypt
1968 Soviet Union invades Czechoslovakia
1968 Tet Offensive in Vietnam
1968 Student riots are widespread in USA and Europe
</td>
<td>
1961 Francis Crick and Sydney Brenner investiga DNA
1963 Vaccine for measles is developed
1964 China explodes an atomic bomb
1965 Philips Records sell cassettes for recorded music
1966 Soviet spacecraft Luna 9 lands on the moon
1967 First heart transplant operation, South Africa
1968 First supertanker launched to transport oil
1969 US astronauts walk on the moon
1970 IBM develops the floppy disc
</td></tr>

<tr><td>1971-1980</td>
<td>
1971 US combat deaths in Vietnam exceed 45,000
1973 US withdraws from Vietnam
1973 Senate Committee hearings on Watergate scandal begin
1974 President Nixon resigns
1975 Khmer Rouge capture Phnom Penh in Cambodia
1976 Mao Ze Dong dies
1978 Red Brigade terrorists murder Italian politician Aldo Moro
1979 Ayatollah Khomeini takes power in Iran
1979 The Soviet Union invades invades Afghanistan
1980 Zimbabwe gains independence
</td>
<td>
1972 Home video-cassette recorders are on sale
1973 USA launches the Skylab space station
1974 US probe Pioneer II reaches Jupiter
1975 First personal computer is marketed in USA
1976 First genetic engineering company Genente forms, USA
1978 Chloroflourocarbons (CFCs) are banned in spraycans, USA
1979 Nuclear plant breaks down on Three Mile Island
1980 The Sony Walkman is launched
</td></tr>

<tr><td>1981-1990</td>
<td>
1981 General Jaruzelski imposes martial law in Poland
1982 Israel invades Lebanon
1983 President Reagan gives backing to Nicaraguan Contras
1984 Indira Ghandhi is assassinated
1985 Famine and civil war continue in Ethiopia
1989 Protestors demonstrate for democracy in Tiananmen Square
1989 Democratic elections are held in USSR
1989 East and West Germany are unified
1990 Democratic elections are held in Poland
1990 Iraq invades Kuwait
</td>
<td>
1981 IBM launches its personal computer
1982 Compact disc players go on sale
1983 US scientists isolate the HIV virus
1984 Genetic finger-printing developed, Britain
1986 Challenger spacecraft explodes
1986 Chernobyl nuclear power station breaks down, Ukraine
1987 First trans-Atlantic fibre optic cable is laid
1988 US Stealth bomber is launched
</td></tr>

<tr><td>1991-1996</td>
<td>
1991 Coalition armed forces launch Desert Storm attack on Iraq
1992 Serb army beseiges Sarajevo in Bosnia-Herzegovina
1992 Bill Clinton is elected US president
1994 Democratic elections are held in South Africa
1996 Russian army defeated in breakaway republic of Chechnya
</td>
<td>
1991 Computer-guided missiles are used in the G War
1992 UN conference on environmental controls, Rio de Janeiro
1993 US astronauts repair the Hubble Space Telesc
1994 The Channel Tunnel between Britain and France is opened
</td></tr>
</table>

Other cultural events

1952	Ingmar Bergman's film *Summer with Monika*
1953	William Burroughs's novel *Junkie*
1953	Arthur Miller's play *The Crucible*
1954	Marlon Brando stars in *On the Waterfront*
1955	Disneyland opens in Anaheim, California
1956	John Ford's film *The Searchers*
1956	Allen Ginsberg publishes *Howl and Other Poems*
1957	Roland Barthes publishes *Mythologies*
1957	Elvis Presley stars in *Jailhouse Rock*
1960	Alfred Hitchcock's film *Psycho*
1961	Michel Foucault publishes *L'Histoire de la folie*
1961	Joseph Heller's novel *Catch 22*
1962	Stanley Kubrick's film *Lolita*
1964	Clint Eastwood stars in *A Fistful of Dollars*
1965	The Rolling Stones sing *Satisfaction*
1967	Jacques Derrida publishes *Of Grammatology*
1967	Jimi Hendrix records *Are You Experienced?*
1968	George Romero's film *Night of the Living Dead*
1969	*Sesame Street* begins on US television
1970	Dario Fo's play *Accidental Death of an Anarchist*
1971	Stanley Kubrick's film *A Clockwork Orange*
1972	Bernardo Bertolucci's film *Last Tango in Paris*
1973	Jean Baudrillard publishes *The Mirror of Production*
1974	Novelist Alexander Solzhenitsyn is expelled from USSR
1974	Abba wins the Eurovision song contest
1976	Umberto Eco publishes *A Theory of Semiotics*
1977	The Sex Pistols record *God Save the Queen*
1978	Edward Said publishes *Orientalism*
1979	Ridley Scott's film *Alien*
1980	Julia Kristeva publishes *The Powers of Horror*
1981	Jacques Lacan dies
1981	Andrzej Wajda's film *Man of Iron*
1982	Thomas Keneally's novel *Schindler's Ark*
1984	Madonna records *Like a Virgin*
1984	James Cameron's film *Terminator*
1987	Oliver Stone's film *Wall Street*
1987	Prince records *Sign of the Times*
1989	Ayatollah Khomeini issues death threat to Salman Rushdie
1990	Luce Irigaray publishes *Culture of Difference*
1990	Thomas Pynchon's novel *Vineland*
1991	Nirvana record *Nevermind*
1992	Spike Lee's film *Malcolm X*
1994	Snoop Doggy Dog record *Doggy Style*
1995	Gillian Anderson and David Duchovny star in *The X Files*
1996	David Cronenberg's film *Crash*

Visual arts

1951	Barnett Newman paints *Vir Heroicus Sublimis*
1951	Picasso paints *Massacre in Korea*
1953	Francis Picabia dies
1954	Henri Matisse dies
1955	Jasper Johns's painting *White Flag*
1956	Jackson Pollock dies
1956	Pop Art seen at *This is Tomorrow* exhibition in London
1957	Situationist International forms
1958	Jasper Johns's first one-man exhibition
1960	Anthony Caro's sculpture *Twenty Four Hours*
1961	Cy Twombly's painting *Bay of Naples*
1962	Andy Warhol's print *Campbell's Soup Cans*
1963	Roy Lichtenstein's painting *Whaam!*
1963	Joseph Beuys's sculpture *Fat Chair*
1965	Le Corbusier dies
1966	Mark di Suvero designs *Peace Tower*, Los Angeles
1966	Edward Kienholz exhibits *State Hospital*
1967	Richard Long makes *A Line Made by Walking*
1969	Martha Rosler begins her series *Bringing the War Home*
1970	Robert Smithson's land art *Spiral Jetty*
1971	Chris Burden's performance *Shoot*
1972	Christo's *Valley Curtain, Colorado*
1973	Picasso dies
1973	Mary Kelly begins *Post Partum Document*
1974	Judy Chicago begins *The Dinner Party*
1976	Leon Golub begins *Mercenaries* series
1976	Cindy Sherman's first solo exhibition, New York
1977	L. Labowitz and S. Lacey perform *In Mourning and in Rage*
1979	Jörg Immendorff exhibits *Café Deutschland* series, Basle
1980	Julian Schnabel's painting *Exile*
1981	Richard Serra's sculpture *Tilted Arc*
1982	Maya Lin's *Vietnam Veterans Memorial*, Washington
1982	Robert Longo's *Corporate Wars: Wall of Influence*
1982	*Zeitgeist* exhibition, Berlin
1985	The NAMES Project AIDS Memorial Quilt is launched
1986	Jean-Michel Basquiat dies
1987	Andy Warhol dies
1987	Barbara Kruger's *I Shop Therefore I Am*
1987	Andres Serrano's *Piss Christ*
1989	*Magiciens de la Terre* exhibition, Paris
1992	Jo Spence dies
1993	*Abject Art* exhibition, New York
1994	*Bad Girls* exhibition, New York
1994	Clement Greenberg dies
1995–96	*Art and Power* Exhibition, London, Barcelona, Berlin

Bibliography

This book draws extensively on ideas and information found in the texts listed in the bibliography. For Chapter One, I am particularly indebted to the writings of George Dimock, Maud Lavin, Linda Nead, and Lisa Tickner. Chapter Two draws on the works of Peter Adam, Roger Griffin, and Noel O'Sullivan. Chapter Three incorporates the arguments of Matthew Cullerne Brown, Wolfgang Holz, and Brandon Taylor. George Roeder's book provided substantial information in Chapter Four, and I have also relied on the works of George Griswold, K.R.M. Short, and James Young. The writings of Lucy Lippard and Hal Foster were particularly useful for Chapter Five.

ONE: REVOLUTION, REFORM, AND MODERNITY, 1900–39

BERMAN, M., *All That is Solid Melts Into Air: The Experience of Modernity* (New York: Simon and Schuster, 1982)

CHIPP, H., *Picasso's Guernica: History, Transformations, Meanings* (Berkeley, Los Angeles and London: University of California Press, 1988)

DIMOCK, G., "Children of the Mills: Re-Reading Lewis Hine's Child-Labour Photographs," *Oxford Art Journal* 16, no. 2 (1993): pp. 37–54

HARRISON, C., and P. WOOD (eds), *Art in Theory 1900–1990: An Anthology of Changing Ideas* (Oxford: Blackwell, 1992)

LAVIN, M., *Cut With The Kitchen Knife: The Weimar Photomontages of Hannah Höch* (New Haven and London: Yale University Press, 1993)

LEPERLIER, F., and D. BATE, *Mise En Scene: Claude Cahun, Tacita Dean, Virginia Nimarkoh* (exh. cat., London: Institute of Contemporary Art, 1994)

LEWIS, H., *Dada Turns Red: The Politics of Surrealism* (Edinburgh: Edinburgh University Press, 1988)

LUNN, E., *Marxism and Modernism: An Historical Study of Lukács, Brecht, Benjamin, and Adorno* (Berkeley, Los Angeles and London: University of California Press, 1982)

NEAD, L., *The Female Nude: Art, Obscenity and Sexuality* (London and New York: Routledge, 1992), see Ch. II. "Redrawing the Lines: 'The Damaged Venus'," for a discussion of Mary Richardson and the British Suffragette movement

NOCHLIN, L., *Realism* (Harmondsworth, Middlesex: Penguin, 1971)

ROCHFORT, D., *Mexican Muralists: Orozco, Rivera, Siqueiros* (London: Laurence King, 1993)

STOURAC, R., *Theatre as a Weapon: Workers' Theatre in the Soviet Union, Germany, and Britain 1917–1934* (London and New York: Routledge, 1986)

TICKNER, L., *The Spectacle of Women: Imagery of the Suffrage Campaign 1907–14* (London: Chatto and Windus, 1987)

TREUHERZ, J. (ed), *Hard Times: Social Realism in Victorian Art* (exh. cat., Manchester: Manchester City Art Gallery, 1987)

TWO: ART, PROPAGANDA, AND FASCISM

Art and Power: Europe Under the Dictators 1930–45 (exh. cat., London: The Haywood Gallery, 1995)

ADAM, P., *The Arts of the Third Reich* (London: Thames and Hudson, 1992)

BARRON, S., (ed) *Degenerate Art: The Fate of the Avant-Garde in Nazi Germany* (Los Angeles: Los Angeles County Museum of Art, 1991)

GAY, P., *Weimar Culture: The Outsider as Insider* (London: Penguin, 1974)

GRIFFIN, R., *The Nature of Fascism* (London and New York: Routledge, 1991)

HINZ, B., *Art in the Third Reich* (trans. R. and R. Kimber, Oxford: Blackwell, 1979)

O'SULLIVAN, N., *Fascism* (London and Melbourne: Dent and Sons, 1983)

TAYLOR, B., and W. VAN DER WILL, *The Nazification of Art: Art, Design, Music, Architecture and Film in the Third Reich* (Winchester: The Winchester School of Art Press, 1990)

THEWELEIT, K., *Male Fantasies II: Psychoanalysing the White Terror* (trans. C. Turner and E. Carter, Cambridge and Oxford: Polity Press in association with Basil Blackwell, 1989)

THREE: PROPAGANDA IN THE COMMUNIST STATE

BOWLT, J. (ed), *Russian Art of the Avant-Garde: Theory and Criticism 1902–1934*, rev. ed. (London: Thames and Hudson, 1988)

CULLERNE BROWN, M., *Art Under Stalin* (Oxford: Phaidon, 1991)

GOLOMSTOCK, I., *Totalitarian Art in the Soviet Union, the Third Reich, Fascist Italy and the People's Republic of China* (trans. R. Chandler, London: Collins Harvill, 1990)

GROYS, B., *The Total Art of Stalinism: Avant-Garde, Aesthetic Dictatorship, and Beyond* (Princeton, N.J.: Princeton University Press, 1992)

JAMES, C. V., *Soviet Socialist Realism: Origins and Theory* (London: Macmillan, 1973)

LINDEY, C., *Art in the Cold War: From Vladivostok to Kalamazoo, 1945–62* (London: The Herbert Press, 1990)

LODDER, C., *Russian Constructivism* (New Haven and London: Yale University Press, 1983)

ROSENFELD, A., and N. T. DODGE (eds), *Nonconformist Art: The Soviet Experience 1956–1986* (New Jersey: The Jane Voorhees Zimmerli Art Museum, Rutgers, in association with Thames and Hudson, 1995)

TAYLOR, B., *Art and Literature Under the Bolsheviks* (London: Pluto Press, vol. 1 1991, vol. 2 1992)

TAYLOR, B., and M. CULLERNE BROWN (eds), *Art of the Soviets: Painting, Sculpture and Architecture in a One-Party State, 1917–1992* (Manchester and New York: Manchester University Press, 1993). For a concise account of Stalinist art, see the essay in this collection by W. Holz, "Allegory and Iconography in Socialist Realist Painting."

TOLSTOY, V., I. BIBIKOVA and C. COOKE (eds), *Street Art of the Revolution: Festivals and Celebrations in Russia 1918–33* (Moscow: Iskusstvo, 1984; London: Thames and Hudson, 1990; New York: Vendome, 1990)

FOUR: PROPAGANDA AT WAR

GRISWOLD, C., "The Vietnam Veterans Memorial and the Washington Mall: Philosophical Thoughts on Political Iconography," in H. SENIE, and S. WEBSTER, *Critical Issues in Public Art: Content, Context and Controversy* (New York: HarperCollins, 1992), pp. 71–100

HIGONNET, M. R., J. JENSON, S. MICHEL, and M. COLLINS WEITZ (eds), *Behind the Lines: Gender and the Two World Wars* (New Haven and London: Yale University Press, 1987)

PARET, P., and B. IRWIN LEWIS, *Persuasive Images: Posters of War and Revolution from the Hoover Institution Archives* (Princeton, N.J.: Princeton University Press, 1992)

RHODES, A., *Propaganda, The Art of Persuasion: World War II* (New York and London: Chelsea House, 1976)

ROEDER, G. H., *The Censored War: American Visual Experience During World War Two* (New Haven and London: Yale University Press, 1993)

SHORT, K.R.M. (ed), *Film and Radio Propaganda in World War Two* (London and Canberra: Croom Helm, 1983)

TAYLOR, P., *War and the Media: Propaganda and Persuasion in the Gulf War* (Manchester and New York: Manchester University Press, 1992)

VIRILIO, P., *War and Cinema: The Logistics of Perception* (trans. P. Camiller, London and New York: Verso, 1989; first published by Cahiers du cinéma/Editions de l'Etoile, 1984)

YOUNG, J., *The Texture of Memory: Holocaust Memorials and Meaning* (New Haven and London: Yale University Press, 1993)

FIVE: THE ART OF PROTEST: FROM VIETNAM TO AIDS

BROUDE, N., and M. GARRARD (eds), *The Power of Feminist Art: The American Movement of the 1970s, History and Impact* (New York: Harry N. Abrams, 1994)

CHADWICK, W., *Women, Art and Society* (London: Thames and Hudson, 1990)

CHANAN, M. (ed), *Twenty-Five Years of the New Latin American Cinema* (London: British Film Institute and Channel Four, 1983)

DUBIN, S., *Arresting Images: Impolitic Art and Uncivil Actions* (London and New York: Routledge, 1992)

FOSTER, H., "Subversive Signs," *Art in America* , 10 (November 1982): pp. 88–93

FRASCINA, F., J. HARRIS, C. HARRISON, and P. WOOD, *Modernism in Dispute: Art Since the Forties* (New Haven and London: Yale University Press, 1993)

FRASCINA, F. (ed), *Pollock and After: The Critical Debate* (London: Harper and Row, and Paul Chapman, 1985)

GADJIGO, S., R. FAULKINGHAM, T. CASSIRER, and R. SANDER, *Ousmane Sembène: Dialogues with Critics and Writers* (Amherst, Mass.: University of Massachusetts Press, 1993)

GUILBAUT, S., *How New York Stole the Idea of Modern Art: Abstract Expressionism, Freedom, and the Cold War* (Chicago and London: The University of Chicago Press, 1983)

LIPPARD, L., *A Different War* [on art and the Vietnam War] (exh. cat., Seattle, Washington: The Real Comet Press and the Whatcom Museum of History and Art, 1990)

LURIE, D. and K. WODICZKO, "Homeless Vehicle Project,", *October*, 47 (Winter 1988): pp. 53–76

Mona Hatoum (exh. cat., Bristol: Arnolfini, 1993)

PLANT, S., *The Most Radical Gesture: The Situationist International in a Postmodern Age* (London: Routledge, 1992)

ROHAN, M., *Paris '68: Graffiti, Posters, Newspapers and Poems of the Events of May 1968* (London: Impact Books, 1988)

SPENCE, J., *Putting Myself in the Picture: A Political, Personal and Photographic Autobiography* (London: Camden Press, 1986)

UKADIKE, N. F., *Black African Cinema* (Berkeley, Los Angeles and London: University of California Press, 1994)

VOGEL, S. and I. EBONG (eds), *Africa Explores: 20th Century African Art* (New York: The Center for African Art, New York, in association with Prestel, 1991)

Picture Credits

Collections are given in the captions alongside the illustrations. Sources for illustrations not supplied by museums or collections, additional information, and copyright credits are given below. Numbers are figure numbers unless otherwise indicated.

Title pages as figure 107 By permission of the artist Rita Donagh, courtesy the British Council, London

1   © DACS 1997

page 7 detail of figure 5

3   © Stuart Franklin/Magnum, London

4   Courtesy Marlborough Fine Art (London) Ltd

6   © ADAGP, Paris and DACS, London 1997

page 17 detail of figure 19

7   By permission of Birmingham Museums and Art Gallery

8   © Photo RMN, Paris

9   Bildarchiv Preussischer Kulturbesitz, Berlin

10   AKG, London/© DACS 1997

11   Courtesy George Eastman House, Rochester, New York

12   AKG, London

13   Stiftung Archiv der Akademie der Künste, Berlin

14   Front page of The Daily Sketch (London), 11 March 1914, The British Library (Newspaper Library)

17   Photo Hermann Kiessling, Berlin/© DACS 1997

19   Bob Schalkwijk, Mexico City

20   CNCA-INBA, Museo Nacional de Arte, Mexico City. Photo Arturo Piera

21   © Succession Picasso/DACS 1997

24   Artothek, Peissenberg, Germany

page 47 detail of figure 25

26   British Film Institute, London

27   The Kobal Collection, London

28   © DACS 1997

29   Artothek, Peissenberg, Germany

30, 36, 37 AKG, London

38   Courtesy Yildiz Film/ZEF Productions Ltd

39   AKG, London, photo Eric Lessing

40, 41 British Film Institute, London

42   Artothek, Peissenberg, Germany

43   Zentralinstitut für Kunstgeschichte, Munich

page 73 detail of figure 47

47   AKG, London/ © DACS 1997

50   © DACS 1997

51, 52 British Film Institute, London

53   Archives of Calmann & King, London

54   Novosti Photo Library, London

55, 56 Novosti Photo Library, London/ © DACS 1997

58   The Bridgeman Art Library, London/ © DACS 1997

59   AKG, London

60   © DACS 1997

62   Novosti Photo Library, London

63   The Bridgeman Art Library, London

64   Jane Voorhees Zimmerli Art Museum, Rutgers, the State University of New Jersey. The Norton and Nancy Dodge Collection from the Soviet Union. Photo by Jack Abraham

65   Jane Voorhees Zimmerli Art Museum, Rutgers, the State University of New Jersey. The Norton and Nancy Dodge Collection from the Soviet Union © 1996 Grisha Bruskin/VAGA, New York, NY. Photo by Jack Abraham

66   The Kobal Collection, London

page 103 detail of figure 75

73   National Archives USA, Still Picture Branch 44-PA-87

74   AKG, London

76   The Ronald Grant Archive, London

77   US Navy/TRH Pictures, London

78   Esto Photographics, Mamaroneck, New York

79   © Peter Marlow/Magnum, London

80, 81 Courtesy the artists

page 125 detail of figure 89

82 & 84 Courtesy the artist and Rhona Hoffman Gallery, Chicago/photograph Michael Tropea, Chicago

Index

Exodus
Chapter 12
Verse 14-20
Page 91-92
- First month of the fourteenth day
- Start from 14th January to 21th January
- Must eat unfermented cakes

Exodus
Chapter 12
Verse 43-49
Page 92-93

Exodus
Chapter 13
Verse 14-16
Page 94

Exodus
Chapter 16
Verses 14- up to chapter 17